The Qumrān Community

THE MACMILLAN COMPANY
NEW YORK • CHICAGO
DALLAS • ATLANTA • SAN FRANCISCO
LONDON • MANILA

**THE MACMILLAN COMPANY
OF CANADA, LIMITED**
TORONTO

THE QUMRĀN COM- MUNITY

Its History and Scrolls

by CHARLES T. FRITSCH

The Macmillan Company, *New York*, 1956

Library of Congress catalog card number: 56-7302

To my Parents

Preface

QUITE BY ACCIDENT on a spring day in 1947 an Arab shepherd came across several manuscripts in a cave on the shore of the Dead Sea. Little did the unsuspecting Bedouin realize that his discovery was to inaugurate a new era in Biblical studies. Since that eventful day more than four hundred manuscripts in varying conditions of preservation have been found in caves of the Qumrān region. In this library are represented all the books of the Old Testament— some many times—Apocryphal works known and unknown, and the sectarian documents of the Jewish monastic sect who lived in the caves and copied their precious manuscripts in the community center which they had built on the plateau near the Sea. After this phenomenal find, the agile, tireless Bedouins discovered at least three other cave sites in the desolate wilderness of Judea which have produced both Biblical and non-Biblical material of unique significance.

It is my purpose to relate these thrilling discoveries and present their significance for Biblical studies in a way that will catch the imagination of the general reader, and at the same time be practical for the student who may wish to pursue the subject more thoroughly. A bibliography of books and articles on the Dead Sea Scrolls and related subjects, from 1953 to the summer of 1955, appears at the end of the book.

To John A. Mackay, President of Princeton Theological Seminary, and to its Board of Trustees, I am deeply grateful for the Sabbatic leave during which I was able to visit the Holy Land and the cave sites in the Judean Desert, and gain first-hand knowledge of the manuscript material in the Palestine Museum, Jerusalem (Jordan). I also wish to express my thanks to Professor Georges A. Barrois, colleague and friend, who read the chapters on the archaeological finds at Khirbet Qumrān and the cave sites, and offered helpful criticisms and suggestions. Without the loyal devotion and encouragement of my wife this book would have never been written. To her I owe an eternal debt of gratitude.

Charles T. Fritsch

Princeton, New Jersey
Summer, 1955

Contents

Preface   vii

I   The Excavations at Khirbet Qumrān   1

II The History of the Qumrān Community   16

III The Caves of Qumrān and the Manuscripts   26

IV Manuscript Discoveries at Khirbet Mird and
    Murabba'at   50

V   The Qumrān Community and the Manuscripts   61

VI The Qumrān Community and the Damascus Sect   76

VII The Qumrān Community and the Essenes   90

VIII The Qumrān Community and the New Testament   111

    Abbreviations   128

    Bibliography   131

    Index   143

Illustrations

The copper scrolls   *facing* 20

Cylindrical jars and covers from the caves at Qumrān   21

A letter of Simeon Bar Kochba, found at Murabba'at   21

Col. VII of the Habakkuk Commentary (1QpHab)   36

A cistern at Qumrān with crack in the steps   52

The table and bench of the Qumrān Scriptorium exhibition
    at the Palestine Archaeological Museum in Jerusalem
    (Jordan)   53

CHAPTER I

The Excavations
at Khirbet Qumrān

ABOUT seven miles south of Jericho on the western shore of the Dead Sea a monastic community, now in ruins, flourished from about 100 B.C. to A.D. 68. The Khirbeh, or ruin, is on a plateau bounded on the east by the Sea and on the west by steep, cave-dotted cliffs, where the members of the community lived, and where they hid their precious manuscripts before the Roman legions destroyed the place in A.D. 68. Flanking the Khirbeh on the south is the Wadi Qumrān, through which during the rainy season rush torrents of water fed by cascades over the steep cliffs. Some of the water is trapped in huge natural cisterns at the base of the escarpment, from which it was directed in ancient times into the community center by a stone aqueduct, traces of which can still be seen. It was only by systematic storage and careful use of this most precious commodity that the community could exist in such a desolate region. To the east of the Khirbeh, separated from it by an esplanade, an enormous cemetery of more than a thousand graves extends down toward the Dead Sea. Archaeological evidence has now definitely established that the caves, the communal center, and the cemetery all were integrally related parts of the Qumrān community which occupied this site for almost two hundred years.

To get to Qumrān today, one must drive from the police post at the head of the Dead Sea a few miles through the trackless wastes to a newly built approach which leads from the coastal

plain to the plateau of the Khirbeh. The new approach, made at
the beginning of the second archaeological campaign in 1953,
follows traces of an ancient roadway which had once been used to
reach the community center from the shore of the Sea. Arriving at
the vantage point of the community center, one has a sweeping
view from Jericho's verdant groves and orchards on the north,
across the deep blue waters of the Dead Sea—guarded at the east
by Moab's barren hills—to the promontory of Ras Feshka, which
juts out to the edge of the Sea several miles farther south.

Since 1850 several travelers and scholars have left us their impres-
sions of Khirbet Qumrān. As early as 1851, Félicien de Saulcy
came to the conclusion that this was the site of ancient Gomorrah.[1]
He held that the name Qumrān was etymologically connected with
Gomorrah—a theory which is linguistically untenable.[2] Clermont-
Ganneau explored this region in 1873–1874 and gave the world
the first valid description of the site. He wrote:

The ruins are insignificant in themselves, consisting of some dilapi-
dated walls of low stones and a small *birkeh* with steps leading to it.
The ground is strewn with numerous fragments of pottery of all descriptions.

If ever there existed there a town properly so called, it must have
been a very small one. . . .

The most interesting feature of Kumrān is the tombs, which, to the
number of a thousand or so, cover the main plateau and the adjacent mounds.[3]

[1] F. de Saulcy, *Voyage autour de la Mer morte* (1853), II, 165–167.
[2] See C. Clermont-Ganneau, *Archaeological Researches in Palestine* (1896),
II, 15, where he strongly repudiates this identification of Qumrān with Gomorrah on every ground. Also F. M. Abel, *Une Croisière autour de la Mer
morte* (Paris, 1911), 167–168. Clermont-Ganneau suggests that Gomorrah
might be connected with Wadi Ghamr which is south of the Dead Sea. Abbé
Milik ("Une Inscription et une lettre en araméen Christo-palestinien," *RB*,
LX [1953], 538, n. 8) believes that the origin of the name Qumrān is to be
found in Calamon, the name given in monastic sources to the coastal plain
of the Dead Sea in the vicinity of the Jordan. R. North states dogmatically
that Qumrān means "lunar," like Jericho ("Qumrân and Its Archaeology,"
CBQ, XVI [1954], 427).
[3] *Op. cit.*, 14–15.

He then goes on to describe in detail the cemetery and a tomb which he opened. G. Dalman, however, was the first to identify the ruins of Qumrān correctly: "Ein Bruchstück eines Säulenfusses, das wir unter den Trümmern fanden, mag gleichwohl für römische oder byzantinische Zeit sprechen. Keine Anzeichen einer alten Ortslage sind vorhanden. Ein Kloster, dem die Kirche nicht fehlen dürfte, ist für diese Gegend nicht überliefert. So wird nur an eine Burg [stronghold] gedacht werden können." [4] Without any evidence of an inhabited area or town, or any tradition of a monastery on the site, he could only reason that the ruins were of a military outpost of Roman times.

Within a few years Khirbet Qumrān has become one of the most interesting sites in Palestine because of the phenomenal manuscript discoveries which have been taking place since 1947 in the caves near by. In 1949, when G. Lankester Harding, Director of the Jordan Government Department of Antiquities, and Père de Vaux, Director of the École Biblique in Jerusalem (Jordan), were exploring Cave 1, where the first manuscripts had been found two years before, their attention was drawn to the ruins on the plateau, about a mile farther south. A preliminary investigation was immediately undertaken, but no evidence was found that the Khirbeh was in any way connected with the manuscript cave.

Not satisfied with this negative conclusion, they decided to excavate the site on the plateau more thoroughly; and the first major archaeological campaign was launched at Qumrān in 1951, between November 24 and December 12.[5] This first digging definitely established that the site was occupied at the same time as the caves, and by the same people; also, that the cemetery was contemporaneous with the site. The general period of occupation

---

[4] G. Dalman, "Chirbet Ḳumrān," *PJB*, X (1914), 10. Cf. also *PJB*, XVI (1920), 40.

[5] R. de Vaux, "Fouille au Khirbet Qumrân: Rapport préliminaire" *RB*, LX (1953), 83–106. The work was carried on under the auspices of the Department of Antiquities of Jordan, the École Biblique, and the Archaeological **Museum of Palestine.**

was ascertained, but later campaigns made possible more accurate dating.

Because of these first important results from archaeological activity at Qumrān, it was decided to carry on the excavation more thoroughly. A second campaign was therefore conducted by the same institutions from February 9 to April 24, 1953.[6] The results were so phenomenal that a third season of excavating was undertaken from February 15 to April 15, 1954. It was my privilege to visit Qumrān several times during this period and to be conducted around the excavations by Père de Vaux himself. So vivid was his description that I could almost see the members of the community eating together in the large dining room, or copying manuscripts in the scriptorium, or scurrying to the caves with their precious library as the Roman Tenth Legion marched down from Jericho to destroy the community.

The following summary of the three seasons of excavating at Qumrān is drawn mainly from the two preliminary reports in *Revue Biblique* and from a public lecture on the third season by Père de Vaux at the École Biblique, June 4, 1954. It may be said that the third season has entirely corroborated the interpretation of the evidence brought to light in the preceding campaigns.

The main building of the community was rectangular, measuring 30 by 37 meters, and was the nucleus of an ever expanding and changing complex of rooms and cisterns. Without describing in detail the changes that took place from one period to another in the community building,[7] it may be observed that its communal character was emphasized as it was extended southward.

The northwest corner of the central structure was occupied by a massive tower with walls more than three feet thick. In the tower were several communicating rooms without windows, except two narrow openings in one wall. Its defensive character is indicated

[6] R. de Vaux, "Fouilles au Khirbet Qumrân: Rapport préliminaire sur la deuxième campagne," *RB*, LXI (1954), 206–236.
[7] The three main periods of occupation of the site, established by texts, pottery, and coinage may be dated approximately as follows: I, 110–31 B.C. (earthquake); II, A.D. 1–68; III, A.D. 68–100.

by the fact that it had no outside door and was isolated from the rest of the building by two uncovered passageways on the east and south sides. The tower was reenforced by stone embankments on all sides probably after the severe earthquake in 31 B.C. That it was used as a bastion of defense to the very last is proved by the discovery in one of its chambers of a cache of coins from the time of the Second Jewish Revolt.

Directly to the east of the tower is a room with several fireplaces which may have served as the kitchen for the community.

The rooms immediately to the southwest of the tower were mainly assembly halls or refectories for the members of the community. The low, carefully plastered bench along the four sides of one of them suggests that it was used as a meeting place by the sect.

Beside this room, at the east, is the largest hall of the main building, where curiously shaped plaster fragments were found in the debris, defying all theories of explanation. With great care they were collected and sent to the Palestine Museum in Jerusalem. There they were patiently assembled, and turned out to be a long, narrow table, a companion bench, and a low, small platform with two shallow depressions hollowed out of the top surface. Now, just what was the purpose of these pieces of furniture found together? This puzzling question was solved by the discovery in the same debris of two inkwells of the Roman period—one of bronze and the other of terra cotta. One of them even contained some dried ink. There is little doubt that this room was the scriptorium where manuscripts were copied by the scribes of the community. Perhaps the scribes used the little platform with the hollowed-out basins for ritual washings while copying the sacred texts.

In the southeast part of the main building have been uncovered two cisterns, several large sinks, and a latrine with a kind of "septic tank." The cisterns, or artificial reservoirs, were carefully constructed and lined with plaster. In one, which is long and very deep, fourteen steps lead down into the pool. The upper steps are railed off into four passages, as though to guide people into the water. The water for these reservoirs was overflow channeled from another large reservoir just outside the southern wall of the main building. All the water for the intricate system of reservoirs, sumps, and connecting canals was brought across the plateau from the natural reservoirs at the base of the cliffs by a stone aqueduct, traces of which can still be seen.

Running diagonally down the fourteen steps just described is a well defined fault, or crack, which must have been caused by a severe earthquake. It can be traced along the floor of the artificially built cistern and through several rooms beyond. Probably the same tremor caused the damage to the tower on the northeast corner of the building.[8] If, as Père de Vaux believes, this clearly visible fault in the reservoir resulted from the earthquake in the spring of 31 B.C. described by Josephus, it is an extraordinary archaeological discovery: excavators do not often uncover such precisely datable evidence of a natural phenomenon.[9]

We cannot stress too much the importance of the reservoirs and the complicated system of canals and sumps discovered in the community center of Qumrān. Water was of course a basic requirement in a desert region, and the number of inhabitants depended entirely on the amount that could be preserved through the long, hot dry season. Four huge open cisterns, together with many smaller reservoirs, have been discovered at Khirbet Qumrān, showing how serious the problem was for the community.

And yet, with each visit to Qumrān, I became more thoroughly convinced that this intricate and complicated water system played a larger role in the community than the satisfaction of ordinary, daily needs. Apart from the staggering number of artificial repositories for water of all shapes and sizes,[10] each of the huge open cisterns has wide steps to the bottom, and the smaller ones have narrower steps leading down along the side. Were these steps used

[8] See above, p. 4.
[9] See below, p. 17 for a full discussion of the problem.
[10] One of the official members of the dig estimated that there were about forty reservoirs.

merely to clean the pools out periodically, or did they have some other purpose? It has already been pointed out that the upper steps of one of the large reservoirs were divided into four parts. In the large pool along the southern wall of the main building, the steps are subdivided into small groups of three or four, with a wider step separating each group from the next. Now, what is the explanation of the different arrangements and groupings of steps into the large reservoirs?

The only plausible answer is that they were used for baptismal or lustration rites. This fits in perfectly with several references in the Qumrān texts to the lustral washings and baptismal rites observed by the members of the community. There was probably an initiatory baptismal rite for the candidate who was admitted into the community after two years' probation. The so-called *Manual of Discipline*, designated as 1QS, seems to refer to this rite when it warns that the unrepentant may not participate:

He may not enter into the water to touch the purity of the holy men, for they will not be cleansed unless they have turned from their wickedness, for uncleanness is in all the transgressors of his word. [V, 13-14.]

Again, it is said that the sinner

cannot purify himself by atonement, nor cleanse himself with water of impurity [i.e., water which takes away impurity], nor sanctify himself with seas or rivers, nor cleanse himself with any water of washing. [1QS, III, 4-5.]

On the other hand, the one whose sins are atoned for by God's spirit

may sprinkle himself with water of impurity and sanctify himself with rippling water. [1QS, III, 9.]

In the *Fragments of a Zadokite Work*, more correctly called *The Cairo Genizah Document of the Damascus Covenanters*, and designated hereafter as CDC,[11] we find rather strict regulations regarding purification with water:

> As to being cleansed in water. No man shall wash in water [that is] filthy or insufficient for a man's bath. None shall cleanse himself in the waters of a vessel. And every pool in a rock in which there is not sufficient [water] for a bath, which an unclean person has touched, its waters shall be unclean like the waters of the vessel. [CDC, XII.] [12]

It would seem then that these texts, which show that the Qumrān community was a baptizing sect, are substantially corroborated by the archaeological evidence from the excavations at Qumrān.

Another large assembly room or refectory which could seat about two hundred people was uncovered to the south of the main building. Just a little off center, near one end of this large hall, is a slightly raised, round podium which calls for explanation. The theory that the room was a refectory, in which one of the members read from the podium during mealtime, is strengthened by the fact that about eleven hundred bowls were found stacked up against the wall of an adjoining room,[13] suggesting that this was a pantry. Then a kitchen also should have been near; but none has been found. The other theory is that the room was the main assembly hall for the community, where the members met as described so graphically in 1QS:

> Now this is the procedure for the session of the many, each in his assigned position: the priests shall sit down first, and the elders, second, and then the rest of all the people shall sit down, each one in his position. And in this order they shall be asked concerning judgment or any other counsel or matter which comes before the many, to answer each one his friend in regard to the counsel of the Community. Let no one speak in the midst of the words of his neighbor, before his brother finishes speaking. And also, let him not speak before his

[11] The citations and translations of this work are taken from R. H. Charles, *The Apocrypha and Pseudepigrapha of the Old Testament in English* (1913), II, 758–834. See below p. 76.
[12] Cf. also the references of Josephus to the purificatory rites of the Essenes in *The Wars of the Jews*, II, vii, 5, and *The Antiquities of the Jews*, XVIII, i, 5.
[13] See below, p. 13, for a more detailed description.

proper order, [i.e., before the one] who is enrolled before him. [VI, 8–11.] [14]

If this room was the assembly hall, then the podium may have been the place from which the Supervisor, or Overseer, presided over the sessions.

In this brief description of the architectural features of the Qumrān community center, a word should be said about significant changes in its plan during the various periods in its two hundred years. The original building, which served as the communal center for the sect from about 110 to 31 B.C., measured 30 to 37 meters. After being severely damaged by an earthquake and being abandoned for years, it was rebuilt and greatly enlarged. The tower walls were reenforced by embankments of rocks; the southeast corner, which had contained the "water works," was turned into an open court; and new reservoirs and rooms, emphasizing the communal character of the sect, were added to the south of the main rectangular structure. The expansion and growth of the community, thus reflected, began about the year 1 and lasted until A.D. 68, when the Romans destroyed the building. They used the site as a military outpost until about the end of the century. The structure they raised on the foundations was utterly different. Large halls were divided into smaller rooms, and the intricate drainage system was replaced by a crudely constructed canal that connected the huge reservoir at the extreme southeast corner of the site with the aqueduct from the wadi. The characteristic communal features of the center had been obliterated in the third period of its history.

The Cemetery

A surprising thing that has attracted the attention of visitors to Qumrān from the earliest times is the cemetery of more than a thousand neatly arranged graves that extends from the center toward the shore. One of the earliest descriptions is by Clermont-Ganneau:

[14] Cf. John 13:24. Also I Cor. 14:30, 40. See below, p. 123.

The most interesting feature of Kumrân is the tombs, which, to the number of a thousand or so, cover the main plateau and the adjacent mounds.

Judging merely by their outward appearance, you would take them to be ordinary Arab tombs, composed of a small oblong tumulus, with its sides straight and its ends rounded off, surrounded by a row of unhewn stones, with one of larger size standing upright at either end. They are clearly distinguished, however, from the modern Mussulman graves by their orientation, the longer axis in every case pointing *north and south*, and not east and west. This very unusual circumstance had already been noticed by the Mussulman guides of M. Rey, who made the same remark as our men, that these were tombs of *Kuffâr*, that is to say unbelievers, non-Mussulmans.

I made up my mind to have one of them opened. Our two men from Selwân set to work before our eyes, and we attentively followed the progress of this small excavation, which presented, I may remark, no difficulty whatever. After going down about a metre, our workmen came upon a layer of bricks of unbaked clay . . . resting on a sort of ledge formed in the soil itself. On removing these bricks we found in the grave proper that they covered the half decayed bones of the body that had been buried there. . . .

There was nothing else whatever to afford any indications. The head was towards the south, the feet towards the north.[15]

Père de Vaux has excavated about twenty graves in various parts of the cemetery. All are of the general type described by Clermont-Ganneau, very simply constructed, with the body usually face upward in a chamber hollowed out directly under one of the long walls of the pit, and sealed off by stones or baked bricks.

The skeletal remains are very fragile, and in many cases they have been crushed by the collapse of the chamber in which they were interred. Parts of nine skeletons were sent for examination to Professor H. V. Vallois, director of the Musée de l'Homme in Paris, who reports that several female skeletons were among them. The presence of women in the community seems to be recognized by the texts of the Order. In CDC, for instance, we read:

[15] Clermont-Ganneau, *op. cit.*, 15–16.

The Builders of the wall who walk after law—the law it is which talks, of which He said: Assuredly they shall talk—are caught (by two) by fornication in taking two wives during their lifetime. But the fundamental principle of creation is "Male and Female created He them." [VII, 1–2.]

An unpublished part of 1QS also refers to women and children.[16] So once again the archaeological evidence from Qumrān corroborates the texts of the community.

The absence of jewelry or ornamental objects in the graves points either to the poverty-stricken condition of the members of the sect, or to a rigid, monastic discipline that did not allow them to wear finery. The absence of funerary offerings is less remarkable than Père de Vaux seems to believe,[17] because most Jewish graves of this time yield practically no such offerings, except ossuaries. Potsherds of the same period as those found in the main building have been discovered in the earth used to fill the graves, showing that the cemetery is of the same age as the adjacent ruins.

In the words of Professor Dupont-Sommer, a fitting tribute to these fallen heroes of Israel: "Here lie these warriors, these wrestlers of God, after the fierce struggle of their lives on earth! The simplicity of the graves reflects the spirit of poverty which inspired them in their lifetime. The regular arrangement of the graveyard reflects the strict discipline of their communal lives, and the uniformity of the tombs is in accordance with their spirit of equality." [18]

Pottery

One of the main factors in determining the history of a site like Khirbet Qumrān is the lowly potsherd. From the shape, size, texture, and coloring of the broken pieces of pottery the trained ceramist can date the various levels of his dig as accurately as though he

---

[16] Josephus tells us that among the Essenes, with whom most scholars identify the Qumrān sect, there was a marrying order. See below, p. 102.

[17] *RB*, LX (1953), 103.

[18] A. Dupont-Sommer, *The Jewish Sect of Qumrân and the Essenes*, transl. by R. D. Barnett (London, 1954), 7–8.

were reading a written record. It is due in large part, therefore, to the countless sherds found at the Khirbeh that we have such an accurate picture of the history of the Qumrān community.

The accidental noting of a few potsherds on the ground about 30 meters north of the ruins led to the discovery of a large number of them, all of which date from the Hellenistic period. On one the letters of the Hebrew alphabet are inscribed. The writing is very poor, and a few letters are missing. About thirty coins also were found in this unstratified material, which Père de Vaux believes may have been debris thrown away when the main building was restored after the earthquake of 31 B.C.

In the main structure, however, it is difficult to distinguish the pottery of level I, corresponding to the first period of the community's history, from that of level II, which corresponds to the second period of the community's history, because many of the pieces were used again in the second period after the restoration of the building. Those that can be definitely established as belonging to level I are identical with the sherds from the debris pile outside the main building, which confirms Père de Vaux's hypothesis.[19]

Of special interest from level I is a small vessel found on the stairs of the reservoir, which had been cracked by the earthquake. It was used to take water from larger vessels—probably, like its Graeco-Roman counterparts, for ceremonial ablutions.

The greatest amount of pottery by far comes from the second period of the community, i.e., from about the year 1 to A.D. 68. The numerous types from this period are clearly related to those of the preceding level. The evolution in lamp forms and in the large cylindrical jars is clearly discernible from one period to the next. Père de Vaux's report on the second season of excavating at Qumrān mentions inscriptions on various pieces of pottery.[20] A name was painted on one tall jar; a pitcher had several Greek let-

[19] For drawings of pottery types from the debris pile and the various levels of the building, see RB, LXI (1954), 215–227.
[20] RB, LXI (1954), 229.

ters on its neck. A terra cotta seal was inscribed with a Greek name. Half a dozen ostraca bearing Hebrew words and letters were discovered in various parts of the excavation. But no manuscript material has been found in the main building.

The third season of excavating revealed a room adjoining the large hall south of the main rectangular unit which had more than eleven hundred bowls stacked along the walls according to sizes and types, some of them with inscriptional material that cannot yet be divulged. A large cylindrical jar, similar to the jars in which the manuscripts from Cave 1 were placed, was found intact in one of the chambers.

Study of the pottery and its stratification at Qumrān not only has revealed the various stages in the history of the community, but also has shown the integral relation between the caves, the center, and the cemetery. The types of pottery discovered at Qumrān are unquestionably from the late Hellenistic and early Roman periods, and the pattern of dating they suggest is as follows: level I, the end of the Hellenistic period; level II, the beginning of the Roman period; level III, a little later. It has also been pointed out that the ceramic material discovered in Cave 1 and in the fill of the graves in the cemetery is of the same general type as that found in the Khirbeh, especially from level II. Thus the lowly potsherd becomes important evidence in determining the date and history of the Qumrān community.

Coinage

Of the 750 coins at Qumrān, not one was discovered in the caves. All were found in the ruins, and it is safe to conjecture that all money transactions took place in the community center, and that the members of the community, who lived in the caves and crevices in the cliffs near by, did not have any coins. This presupposes a common ownership of goods, as well as a rigid discipline of poverty. Here again the excavations at Qumrān accurately illustrate the texts of the Order, for when a neophyte became a mem-

ber of the group "his wealth and his property they shall bring to the
man who is the Supervisor of the property of the many, and he shall
enter it to his credit, but shall not spend of it for the many." (1QS,
VI, 19–20; cf. also VII, 25, and CDC, XVIII.)

Of the coins found at Qumrān during the first two seasons of
excavating [21] a large number are of the Hasmonean period, beginning with John Hyrcanus (135–104 B.C.); only one is of the time
of Herod the Great (37–4 B.C.); many are of the time of Herod
Archelaus (4 B.C. to A.D. 6) and the Roman Procurators down to
the First Jewish Revolt (A.D. 66–70); some are of the second year
of the First Jewish Revolt; a few are from Caesarea and Dora
under Nero—one, marked with an X, belonging to the Tenth Legion; three, with the inscription *Judaea Capta*, are of the period
after the fall of Jerusalem in A.D. 70; and about a dozen date from
the Second Jewish Revolt (A.D. 132–135).

The Hasmonean coins came mostly from the first level of the
Khirbeh and from the debris pile outside the main building; the
coins of A.D. 1–100 were found mainly in the second level, except
those of the period after the First Jewish Revolt, which were found
in level III. The historical spread of the coins, and their distribu-
tion in the various levels of the Khirbeh, confirm precisely the conclusions reached by study of the pottery. Therefore, coins, pottery,
and architectural changes in the main building at Qumrān tell
the same story of the Jewish sectarians who lived there: in brief,
the site was occupied from about 110 B.C. in the reign of John
Hyrcanus until the time of Herod the Great (37–4 B.C.). Then it
was abandoned, and about this time the earthquake severely damaged the main edifice. Restored and enlarged about the year 1, it
was occupied until its final destruction by the Romans in A.D. 68.
Through the rest of the first century the Romans used the site for
a military outpost. According to numismatic evidence, Jewish revolutionaries occupied the site during the Second Jewish Revolt
(132–135), after which it was permanently abandoned. The next
chapter will discuss the history in more detail.

[21] *RB*, LXI (1954), 230.

Other Objects

The fragments of glass found at Qumrān are insignificant. Père de Vaux describes a stone vase in one of his lists of ceramic material.[22] Fragments of large, finely carved basins, as well as of bases and columns were found in the debris of the rooms. They must have belonged to some monumental structure which formed part of the building, or was attached to it. Parts of a large mill for grinding grain were found in different rooms.

Among the metal objects are nails from a door that had collapsed and fallen to the ground in one of the rooms; also a small bronze pail with an iron handle, and several agricultural implements. Iron arrowheads, found in several parts of the building, point to the warlike action which destroyed the community in A.D. 68.

[22] *RB*, LX (1953), 99, No. 12.

CHAPTER II

The History
of the Qumrān Community

FROM the evidence of the ruined community center at Qumrān and of the pottery and coins discovered there, as published in the preliminary reports, it is possible to construct its history with some definiteness. More archaeological campaigns at Qumrān are planned and they will undoubtedly produce new evidence; but there is little likelihood that the general outline presented in this chapter will be altered in a major way.

According to Père de Vaux the discovery at Qumrān of Iron Age potsherds and remnants of an Israelite wall indicates that the site may have been occupied as early as the eighth century B.C. This early occupation perhaps was connected with the widespread activities of Uzziah, king of Judah, who "built towers in the desert, and digged many wells: for he had much cattle, both in the low country, and in the plains" (II Chron. 26:10).[1]

That the major period of occupation began during the reign of John Hyrcanus I (135–104 B.C.) is indicated by the appreciable numbers of coins from this period in the excavation.[2] Similar evidence further establishes that the site continued to be occupied as late as the last Hasmonean ruler, Antigonus Mattathias (40–37 B.C.). Then there was a distinct break in the occupation. The fact

---

[1] Unpublished reports of ceramic evidence from the same period in neighboring desert sites seem to indicate that there was much activity in this region in early times.

[2] See above, p. 14.

that only one lone coin from the long reign of Herod the Great (37–4 B.C.) has been discovered at Qumrān suggests that the site was not occupied during his time.

From the combined evidence of pottery, changes in structure of the monastery, and, of course, coins, it is clear that the damage by earthquake to the main building of the community occurred at the close of this first period. Josephus substantiates this conclusion by describing a severe earthquake in the seventh year of Herod's reign (31 B.C.), when he was at war with the Nabateans:

> At this time it was that the fight happened at Actium, between Octavius Caesar and Antony, in the seventh year of the reign of Herod; and then it was also that there was an earthquake in Judea, such a one as had not happened at any other time, and which earthquake brought a great destruction upon the cattle in that country. About ten thousand men also perished by the fall of houses; but the army, which lodged in the field, received no damage by this sad accident. [*AJ*, XV, v, 2. Cf. also *WJ*, I, xix, 3.]

Josephus then goes on to tell how Herod rallied his forces by an impassioned speech and led them into Trans-Jordan where they scored a smashing victory over their enemies. The earthquake, therefore, that terrified Herod's troops, camped on the plain of Jericho, was the same one that damaged the tower and cisterns of the community center at Qumrān.

Coins struck during the reign of Herod Archelaus (4 B.C. to A.D. 6) indicate reoccupation of the site. The same general plan prevailed as in the first period, and it may be concluded that the center was restored and enlarged by the group that had used it before the earthquake. Coins from the second year of the First Jewish Revolt, A.D. 67–68, date the fiery end of the second period of the community.

That the center was destroyed by the Romans is clear from the numismatic evidence found in the Khirbeh, as well as from Josephus, who wrote in *The Wars of the Jews* that in the spring of A.D. 68, Vespasian set out with the Tenth Legion from Caesarea on the Mediterranean, to finish the conquest of Palestine. Idumea, Samaria, and finally Jericho fell before him, leaving Jerusalem an easy prey for attack. It was while he was encamped on the plains of Jericho that [according to Josephus] he conducted an experiment to prove the unusual qualities of the waters of the Dead Sea about which he had heard.

The nature of the lake Asphaltitis is also worth describing. It is, as I have said already, bitter and unfruitful. It is so light or thick that it bears up the heaviest things that are thrown into it; nor is it easy for any one to make things sink therein to the bottom, if he had a mind so to do. Accordingly, when Vespasian went to see it, he commanded that some who could not swim, should have their hands tied behind them, and be thrown into the deep when it so happened that they all swam as if a wind had forced them upwards. [WJ, IV, viii, 4.]

Fortunately for these poor victims, all that had been said about the Dead Sea proved to be true.

It must have been at the time of the fall of Jericho that the community center at Qumrān was taken by the Roman soldiers. A layer of burnt ash and the presence of iron arrowheads in the Khirbeh point to the sudden end of the community. And in the ruins coins from Caesarea and one marked with an "X" indicate the presence of the Roman Tenth Legion. What happened to the members of the community, we cannot say. Perhaps all were killed, or perhaps some escaped. At any rate, they hid their precious library of manuscripts in the near-by caves.

Leaving a garrison at Jericho, Vespasian returned to Caesarea to prepare for the final assault upon Jerusalem. But the death of Nero in Rome gave him more important matters to think about, and he committed the continuation of the war in Palestine to his son Titus. Among the legions that assembled for the attack on Jerusalem in A.D. 69 was the Tenth, which, according to Josephus, came up from Jericho.[3]

[3] WJ, V, i, 6.

After destroying the monastic center in A.D. 68, the Romans used the site for a military outpost until about the end of the century. Evidence of this third period of occupation comes from several sources. As has been noted, the complete change in character of the main structure shows that the new occupants of the site had no need for the large communal rooms and the complicated water system with numerous cisterns and reservoirs. The obvious inference is that they were Romans, who used the site as a military outpost to watch over the northern half of the Dead Sea. The inference is substantiated by the coins found in the third level of the excavation. Coins from Caesarea and Dora dated in the years 67–68, as well as one marked with an "X," indicated the Tenth Legion. These obviously belonged to Vespasian's troops who had made their way from Caesarea on the Mediterranean down the Jordan valley to the Dead Sea, destroying and plundering everything in preparation for the assault upon Jerusalem. That the Romans remained at Qumrān a number of years is proved by the discovery of three coins marked *Judaea Capta*, which date from the reign of Titus (A.D. 79–81).

The last phase in the history, entirely unrelated to the preceding occupations, has to do with the Second Jewish Revolt, A.D. 132–135. Thirteen coins from this period, found at the bottom of the tower where the Jewish patriots made their last stand, indicate that the Jews used the site as a stronghold in their last futile attempt to oust the Romans from their country. Thereafter Qumrān knew only Arab shepherds who passed with their flocks on the way to the cooling waters of 'Ain Feshka.

The following is a résumé of the history based on the available archaeological and textual evidence:

1. Indications of Israelite occupation, in the eighth century B.C., unrelated to the community.
2. The community.
    a. Construction under John Hyrcanus I (135–104 B.C.). Abandoned at or before severe earthquake in spring of 31 B.C.

b. Restoration under Herod Archelaus (4 B.C. to A.D. 6). Destroyed in June, A.D. 68.

c. Occupied by Roman forces until about the end of first century after Christ.

3. Reoccupied by Jewish partisans during the Second Jewish Revolt (A.D. 132–135).

4. Sporadic, temporary encampments in later times, indicated by a few Byzantine and Arab coins.

The history of the sect that lived here almost two hundred years now becomes clear. For reasons to be discussed later, this sect moved out into the wilderness and built the community center by the Dead Sea some time during the reign of John Hyrcanus I. Here the members ate and studied together, and held their meetings, or "sessions." They buried their dead in the cemetery to the east, and lodged in the caves and crevices in the cliffs near by. In austere simplicity and rigorous discipline the members occupied this desolate spot until the reign of Herod the Great (37–4 B.C.), when they seem to have abandoned the site for almost forty years.[4]

This abandonment of Qumrān is one of the puzzling problems in its history.[5] Why should the members of the sect abandon their elaborately constructed community center during the reign of Herod the Great? The earthquake which severely damaged it in the spring of 31 B.C. has been suggested as the reason; but an earthquake alone would hardly have been sufficient reason for an abandonment lasting almost forty years. We believe that the sectarian documents throw some light upon this mystery, and that Herod himself may have had something to do with the flight from Qumrān.

In 1910 Solomon Schechter published several fragments which had been discovered among many others in the genizah of a syna-

---

[4] During this first period of occupation, from about 110 to 37 B.C., the activities of the Teacher of Righteousness took place, as described in CDC and the Habakkuk Commentary (1QpHab).

[5] Père de Vaux deduces the abandonment from the fact that only one coin of the time of Herod the Great has been found in the Khirbeh. See *RB*, LXI (1954), 235–236.

The copper scrolls

Cylindrical jars and covers from the caves at Qumrān

A letter of Simeon Bar Kochba, found at Murabba'at

gogue in Cairo under the title, *Fragments of a Zadokite Work.*[6]
The close relation of this document to the sectarian scrolls from
Qumrān is now accepted by most scholars, not only because it is
similar in style and terminology but also because the sect described
in the Zadokite work resembles the Qumrān community so strikingly in organization and teachings. The Zadokite document
mentions several times the fact that the sect migrated to Damascus.
"The well is the law, and they who digged it are the penitents of
Israel who went forth out of the land of Judah and sojourned in
the land of Damascus, all of whom God called Princes" (VIII,
6).[7] The leader of the migration to Damascus was called "the
Star," and he organized his followers there into the Community
of the New Covenant.

Now if the sect described in the Zadokite document and the
Qumrān community are one and the same the only conclusion to
be drawn from the above references is that the community at
Qumrān at one time left the Dead Sea and migrated to Damascus.
Why this migration should be denied and Damascus explained as
a purely symbolic term, is a little hard to understand.[8] Nowhere,
as far as I am aware, is Damascus ever used in a symbolic way for
a place of refuge or captivity. On the other hand, it is definitely
known that Damascus and its environs served as a haven for various individuals and groups down through the centuries.[9] Until we

[6] S. Schechter, ed. and transl., *Documents of Jewish Sectaries* (2 vols.,
Cambridge, 1910), Vol. I (*Fragments of a Zadokite Work*). R. H. Charles
published the same material in *Apocrypha and Pseudepigrapha of the Old
Testament in English* (2 vols., Oxford, 1913), Vol. II, 785–834 ("Fragments
of a Zadokite Work"). Citations here are from the Charles edition. Cf. Chap.
VI, following, "The Qumrān Community and the Damascus Sect."
[7] Cf. also VI, 1, and the references to Damascus in VIII, 15, and IX, 5,
8, 28, 37.
[8] Cf. I. Rabinowitz, "A Reconsideration of 'Damascus' and '390 Years' in
the 'Damascus' ('Zadokite') Fragments," *JBL*, LXXIII (1954), 11–35.
[9] Absalom fled to Geshur, an Aramaean kingdom, after slaying his brother
Amnon (II Sam. 13:37–38). Cf. also I Kings 11:24. Because of easy communi-
cation between Damascus and Jerusalem, Christian refugees fled to Damascus
early and established a community (cf. Acts 9:2). It also became a strong
Karaite center in the eighth century and after. At the end of the fifteenth
century a large number of Spanish Jews migrated to Damascus (*Jewish En-
cyclopaedia*, article "Damascus").

have definite proof, then, that there was no migration of this sect to Damascus, we maintain that the Zadokite document refers to a real migration of the sect to a real city, the city of Damascus.

When did this migration of the Qumrān community take place? The only possible time was during the reign of Herod the Great (37-4 B.C.) according to the present interpretation of the archaeological evidence.

If this interpretation is correct, the first question that naturally arises is whether Herod the Great had anything to do with the migration. From Herod's demonstrated character, we may be sure that he had little sympathy with the moral principles and Messianic hopes of the Essene group a few miles from his palace at Jericho. Their strict discipline and high standards of conduct must have been a constant rebuke to his ungovernable passion and sensuality.[10]

Then, too, it must be remembered that Herod the Great was no Jew. His love for Greek culture and his disdain for Jewish laws and regulations made him especially hated among the Pharisees, the "straitest sect of our religion" (Acts 26:5). To be sure, he never openly broke with them, and he even made certain concessions to their strict principles,[11] but these acts of deference never lessened their bitter hatred and loathing for him. Even when he was in the death throes of a horrible disease, "two of the most eloquent men among the Jews, and the most celebrated interpreters of the Jewish laws," stirred up an insurrection against him, inciting the people to pull down "all those works which the king had erected contrary to the law of their fathers." [12] But the plot failed, and the instigators were burned alive.

In the light of the animosity between this profligate Idumean

---

[10] One is reminded, of course, of the clash between John the Baptist and the later Herod Antipas, recorded in the synoptic Gospels: Matt. 14:1-12; Mk. 6:14-29; Luke 9:7-9. John had rebuked him for marrying his brother's wife, and was imprisoned and later beheaded for reasons attributable to Herod's sensual nature.

[11] Cf. AJ, XV, i, 1, and x, 4.

[12] Ibid., XVII, vi, 2.

and the Pharisees, we may well imagine how he regarded the Essenes, who were even more extreme in their views than the Pharisees. They had solved the practical problem of living under the Torah by withdrawing from the world and forming ascetic communities like the one at Qumrān. Here they observed strict rules of conduct, reading and studying the Torah day and night. Certainly nothing could have been more irritating to Herod than to have a community of these pious, Jewish monks within a stone's throw of his Jericho palace; and certainly nothing could have been more repulsive to the puritanical keepers of the Law than the utterly pagan and licentious life of Herod and his court. Whether he and his pious neighbors ever came to blows we do not know; but we know that they could not tolerate "coexistence" with such a corrupt regime, and so they left for a healthier clime to the north.

Another thing which may have irked Herod was the military character of this sect. Its community center was guarded by a strong tower which endured to the very end. Of even greater significance is the fact, according to the *War Scroll*, that the members of this community thought of themselves as the army of the Lord, and had numerous banners and a complicated military organization. The Scroll may be interpreted apocalyptically as referring to the victorious struggle of the children of light with the children of darkness; nevertheless, the minute description of ranks and military procedures seems to indicate that the members of the sect took the militant aspect of their life very seriously, at least at some stage in their history. If Herod came to regard it as a warlike Jewish sect with fanatical Messianic hopes that had serious political implications, he was not the man to tolerate its existence long, especially in the shadow of his own palace.

Finally, the Messianic teachings of the sect may have caused serious friction between Herod and the community. Of course, Herod was an unpredictable, irascible genius, and stopped at nothing to destroy any one who stood in the way of his political aspirations. His Jewish enemies—even the aged Hyrcanus II, who he thought was contriving against him, and members of his family

—were put to the sword at the slightest suspicion of intrigue. So insanely jealous a man, who lived in constant fear of court revolt or popular uprising, would hardly allow at Qumrān, on his very door-step, a community of believers who held that the Messiah from Aaron and Israel was to come through them.[13] They believed that through their Covenant community the ideals of the Messianic Age were to be realized.[14] In view of what this same Herod did when he heard about Him "that is born King of the Jews" (Matt. 2:1–18), we may well understand feelings that would prompt him to banish from his realm a community with such extreme apocalyptic views.[15]

For the reasons just stated, we believe that the break in the occupation of the site at Qumrān—which took place, according to archaeological evidence, during the reign of Herod the Great—corresponds to the Damascus migration of the sect mentioned in CDC, and that the migration to Damascus was due directly to Herod's disapproval of the Order and its teachings.[16]

After the death of Herod, the members of the community re-turned to Qumrān and restored and enlarged their main building.

---

[13] Cf. CDC, II, 9–10, and XI, 30. Also 1QS, IX, 11.

[14] See especially 1QS, VIII, 5–10, and IV, 15–23.

[15] Josephus tells us in AJ, XV, x, 4–5, that Herod held the Essenes (with whom the members of the Qumrān community are probably to be identified) in high regard. "He endeavored also to persuade Pollio the Pharisee, and Sameas, and the greatest part of their scholars to take the oath; but these would neither submit so to do, nor were they punished together with the rest, out of the reverence he bore to Pollio. The Essenes also, as we call a sect of ours, were excused from this imposition. . . . However, it is but fit to set down here the reasons wherefore Herod had these Essenes in such honor, and thought higher of them than their mortal nature required." Then follows the story of how Manahem, an Essene, upon seeing Herod when he was a child, predicted that he was going to be king. Because of this prophecy, Herod "continued to honor all the Essenes." This whole story, and its implications, should probably be taken with a large grain of salt, however, for the following reasons. In the first place, Josephus may not have been aware of all the facts. Herod had good reasons to hate the Qumrān sect, as pointed out above. In the second place, the story that Josephus relates as the reason for Herod's respect for the Essenes sounds like one of those superstitious tales for which Josephus had a special liking. And, thirdly, Josephus tries to portray Herod in a favorable light wherever possible.

[16] For another view, see R. North, "The Damascus of Qumrān Geography," PEQ, LXXXVI (1955), 34–48.

Here they continued their strict, communal, monastic life until the Romans destroyed it in A.D. 68. Before the final destruction, however, the members of the Order hid their precious manuscripts in the caves near by and thus saved them. Some of the large earthen jars in which they placed the manuscripts have been found intact, but most have come down to us in very fragmentary condition. It seems, however, that the large number of manuscripts found in Cave 4, near the Khirbeh, were deposited there hastily; there is no evidence that these were put into receptacles. As a result, they have been reduced to shreds by rats. This hasty disposal of the manuscripts obviously reflects the last-minute activity of the community to save its literary treasures before the Romans conquered Qumrān.

The Caves of Qumrān
and the Manuscripts

EVER since the startling discovery in 1947 of manuscripts in a cave near Khirbet Qumrān, the cliffs along the north-western shore of the Dead Sea and the whole desert region of Judea have been scoured for new manuscript material. In the vanguard of the prospectors have been the Bedouins, suddenly aware of treasures hidden in the caves and crevices of their desert domain. They know every foot of it like a book, and their agility and physical stamina allow them to explore the most inaccesssible places with the greatest of ease. They have discovered all the major manuscript deposits. It is believed that most of this material has reached competent hands, or is now being purchased from the Bedouins for study in the Palestine Museum at Jerusalem.

As the Bedouins discovered cave sites one after another, expeditions went out, mainly under the auspices of the Department of Antiquities of Jordan, the École Biblique in Jerusalem, and the Archaeological Museum of Palestine, to corroborate the reports and to search for material that might have been overlooked. A brief chronological survey of the discoveries in the caves in the Qumrān area by these various expeditions follows.

An expedition under the direction of Père de Vaux and Mr. Lankester Harding set out in the spring of 1949 to explore thoroughly the cave which had yielded the first phenomenal find. The time lag of two years since the first discovery of manuscripts was due to unsettled conditions in Palestine.[1] In the spring of 1952 Père de Vaux and Professor W. L. Reed of the American School of Oriental Research in Jerusalem with a small expedition explored the vicinity of Khirbet Qumrān. They covered an area of about six miles in the rocky escarpment between Hajar al-Asbah to the north and Râs Feshka to the south in order to determine the extent of the area inhabited by the Qumrān sect, and to discover, if possible, more manuscripts which might have been hidden in this region.[2] As a result of this expedition, two more manuscript-bearing caves were discovered: Cave 2, a short distance south of Cave 1, and Cave 3, a little more than a mile north of Cave 1.[3]

In the summer of 1952 the Bedouins found a hole dug in the side of the wadi near the community center, containing thousands of manuscript fragments. (Much of this material is still in the hands of the Ta'amireh tribe, but every effort is being made to purchase all of it before it is sold to outsiders and scattered abroad.) In September, when the find became known, the Jordan authorities undertook a systematic excavation of the site. The material from this cave in the plateau, known as Cave 4, together with the tremendous hoard of fragments that the Bedouins have been selling box by box, is by far the most important find in the Qumrān area. Near Cave 4 the official expedition discovered some badly damaged fragments in another chamber—Cave 5—the only manuscript repository discovered first by archaeologists.[4] Finally, the Bedouins

---

[1] For the original reports of this expedition, see R. de Vaux, "Post-Scriptum: La Cachette des manuscrits hébreux," *RB*, LVI (1949), 234–237, and "La Grotte des Manuscrits Hébreux," *ibid.*, 586–609. Also, O. R. Sellers, "Excavations of the 'Manuscript' Cave at 'Ain Fashka," *BASOR*, No. 114 (1949), 5–9.

[2] For the original reports on this expedition, see R. de Vaux, "Exploration de la région de Qumrān," *RB*, LX (1953), 540–561. Also W. L. Reed, "The Qumrān Caves Expedition of March, 1952," *BASOR*, No. 135, Oct., 1954, 8–13.

[3] For a full description of this expedition, see pp. 38–42.

[4] For brief reports on this expedition, see R. de Vaux, "Fouille au Khirbet Qumrān: Rapport préliminaire," *RB*, LX (1953), 86. Also F. M. Cross, Jr., "The Manuscripts of the Dead Sea Caves," *BA*, XVII (1954), 8. For full description of this material, see pp. 43–46 following.

again came across fragments in a hole in the rocky cliff at the head of the wadi bed, known as Cave 6. The find was important, because among the fragments was a passage of the Zadokite Work (CDC) which has been thought to be related to the Qumrān sectarian works ever since they were discovered in 1947.

The exploration of other cave sites in the Judean desert— Murabba'at in early 1952, Khirbet Mird in the summer of 1952 and again in 1953, and an undetermined site in the summer of 1952— is discussed in Chapter IV. Now follows a description of the Qumrān caves, their exploration, and an inventory of the material found in them.

Cave 1 (1Q)

Cave 1, a little less than a mile north of the community center of Qumrān, was discovered one day in the spring of 1947 by Muḥammad Dib (Muḥammad the Wolf), a shepherd of the Ta'amireh tribe, as he climbed the cliffs looking for a lost sheep. He threw a stone that entered a hole in the rocks and made a strange sound that frightened him away. Returning with a friend to investigate, he discovered a rocky chamber and in it large, tall jars, broken pottery, and the leather scrolls which came to be known as the "Dead Sea Scrolls" or more accurately now the Qumrān Manuscripts.[5]

How the manuscripts got into the hands of scholars during the "days of the trouble" in Palestine is an oft-told tale, full of intrigue and bitter controversy.[6] Of the eleven scrolls, five were purchased by the Syrian Orthodox Convent of St. Mark in Jerusalem, and the remaining six by the Hebrew University. The Syrian-owned manuscripts eventually came to the American School of Oriental Research in Jerusalem, where scholars studied and photographed them under the most trying conditions during the hostilities between Jews and Arabs. Spirited to safety outside Palestine,

---

[5] For another story of the discovery of the 1Q manuscripts, see R. North, "Qumrân and Its Archeology," *CBQ,* XVI (1954), 428.

[6] For the original accounts of these first finds from 1Q and how they got into scholars' hands, see the articles in *Biblical Archaeology,* beginning with May, 1948.

these scrolls were finally brought to America, where they were hidden away in a bank vault. An item in the *New York Times* from Jerusalem, February 13, 1955, reports the purchase of the scrolls in New York for Israel, from Mar Athanasius Y. Samuel, Metropolitan of St. Mark's Syrian Orthodox Convent in Jerusalem, to be "exhibited in a special hall in Jerusalem, to be called the Shrine of the Book, which will be part of the library wing of the Hebrew University buildings now under construction." It is estimated that they were sold for almost $300,000. So once again all the manuscripts discovered in Cave 1 will be together in the land and among the people that gave them birth two thousand years ago.

Before describing the manuscripts from 1Q, it may be well to discuss the excavation which took place two years after the discovery. When the work on Cave 1 at Qumrān was started in the spring of 1949, it was soon discovered that clandestine excavators had visited the place a few months before. The floor of the cave had been dug up to a depth of several inches. Cigarette stubs and a lighter, scraps of newspaper, and other pieces of incriminating evidence were left behind in the debris by these modern marauders, whose identity later became known. They had even made a larger opening into the cave at floor level for easier access. In spite of this unauthorized intrusion, the official excavators found many interesting remains, in three categories.

First, a considerable quantity of cloth was found which presumably had been used to wrap the scrolls when they were put into the jars, because pieces of manuscript material still stuck to the cloth, which proved to be native Palestinian linen. A radiocarbon test showed that it could be dated anywhere between 168 B.C. and A.D. 233.[7] Although the test does not give a precise date, and although the date of the cloth by no means proves the date of the manuscripts, it is one more piece of evidence that points to the early date of the manuscripts.

Secondly, many of the potsherds found are unmistakably of the

[7] O. R. Sellers, "Radiocarbon Dating of Cloth from the 'Ain Feshka Cave," BASOR, No. 123 (1951), 24–26.

late Hellenistic period, i.e., the first century B.C. Pieced together, they form about fifty cylindrical, earthenware jars—on the average a little over two feet high and about ten inches in diameter—and the small bowls that were used to cover them. The first theory was that jars of this previously unknown type were made especially to hold the manuscripts found in them; but it has become clear that they were used in daily life because scores have been found in the caves near by, and one intact in the community center itself. Two Hellenistic lamps have been found in the cave. Besides the Hellenistic ware there are a few fragments from the Roman period, among them two Roman lamps and a cooking pot, indicating that some one broke into the cave during that period. Many scholars connect the intrusion with the well attested story of Origen that certain Greek and Hebrew manuscripts were found in a jar near Jericho during the reign of Caracalla (A.D. 211–217).[8] Because Roman pottery was in the cave, and because originally many more manuscripts were in the cave than the few that have been found, it may well be that some scrolls were removed in Origen's time, perhaps even by Origen himself.

Thirdly, more than six hundred manuscript fragments, of numerous texts, have been discovered in the cave. Investigation brings out that some of the fragments are of scrolls said to have been found in this cave in 1947, thus proving the authenticity of the manuscripts. Fragments of Genesis, Exodus, Leviticus, Deuteronomy, Judges, and Jubilees have now been recognized, as well as some *peshers*,[9] or commentaries on Biblical books, and Aramaic fragments of extracanonical works. Several of these have been published by Père de Vaux [10] because of their special interest for the Old Testament scholar. The first group includes several short passages from Leviticus 19–22, written in the old Hebrew script. Père de Vaux dates these fragments from the fourth century B.C., although Pro-

---

[8] See P. E. Kahle, *The Cairo Geniza* (London, 1947), 160–164, for translation and discussion of the original texts.

[9] J. T. Milik, "Fragments d'un midrash de Michée dans les manuscrits de Qumrān," *RB*, LIX (1952), 412–418.

[10] *RB*, LVI (1949), 597–609.

fessor W. F. Albright thinks that they may have been written as late as the second or preferably early first century B.C., because the writing has "many striking points of contact with the archaizing script of the Maccabaean coins." [11] Another interesting fragment published by Père de Vaux is a small part of the Book of Jubilees, written in Hebrew. It is important, first, because it opens up again the whole question of the language in which the Book of Jubilees was written. De Vaux thinks that this fragment confirms the view that the book was written in Hebrew. Professor Torrey, holding that Jubilees was written in Aramaic, welcomes it as another example of "inter-Semitic translation" which was so common in the intertestamental period: "We are gradually learning that the practice of translating from Hebrew into Aramaic, and from Aramaic into Hebrew, was more common than we had supposed." [12] This fragment is important also because its presence in Cave 1 at Qumrān shows that the library of the sect contained the Book of Jubilees. For reasons which will be discussed below, it is clear that the Jewish sect who took up residence by the Dead Sea produced both Jubilees and the Book of Enoch.

Of the large number of unidentifiable fragments, Père de Vaux has published one which describes the final consummation when wickedness will be wiped out and universal righteousness will prevail.[13]

The Palestine Museum in Jerusalem, according to later reports, purchased more fragments from Cave 1 from the dealer in Bethlehem who had received the first scrolls [14]—among them, two columns from the Manual of Discipline (1QS), which it has put on

[11] *The Old Testament and Modern Study*, ed. H. H. Rowley (Oxford, 1951), 24. On the Leviticus fragments, cf. also S. A. Birnbaum and S. Yeivin in *BASOR*, No. 118 (1950), 20–27, 28–30.

[12] C. C. Torrey, "A Hebrew Fragment of Jubilees," *JBL*, LXXI (1952), 39–41.

[13] For a new translation of this fragment and further comments upon it, see I. Rabinowitz, "The Authorship, Audience and Date of the de Vaux Fragment of an Unknown Work," *JBL*, LXXI (1952), 19–32.

[14] R. de Vaux, "A propos des manuscrits de la Mer morte," *RB*, LVII (1950), 417–429.

display. They seem to be the opening columns of the Manual, since the first starts with the phrase, "And this is the rule." Continuing, the fragment touches on women in the sect, and the young people who are to be brought up on the knowledge of the Book of Hagu—a term found in CDC. It also mentions that the Messiah of Israel is present at the ritual meals of the community.[15] It is hoped that all these manuscript fragments from Cave 1 will soon be published.

The Scrolls Published by the American Schools of Oriental Research

We have already noted that Mar Athanasius Y. Samuel, Metropolitan of St. Mark's Orthodox Convent in Jerusalem, purchased one part of the original cache of manuscripts from Cave 1 at Qumrān (1Q). This group of five scrolls, two being parts of the same manuscript, includes a full-length copy of the Book of Isaiah except a few small lacunae, a sectarian document usually referred to as the Manual of Discipline, an incomplete "commentary" on the Book of Habakkuk, and a scroll which has not yet been unrolled. The group has now been purchased for Israel, which will exhibit it in the library wing of the Hebrew University. Three of these scrolls have now been published.[16]

The Isaiah scroll (1QIs[a]) is of course the most sensational of the manuscript finds from Qumrān, antedating by a millennium or more the oldest known Hebrew texts on which present Biblical translations are based. It consists of fifty-four columns of beautifully preserved Hebrew writing inscribed on seventeen sheets of coarse parchment, which were sewed together to form a scroll more than twenty-four feet long and about ten inches high. The writing averages twenty-nine lines to the column, and the letters are sus-

[15] See D. Barthélemy, "Notes en marge de publications récentes sur les manuscrits de Qumrān," RB, LIX (1952), 187–218.
[16] M. Burrows, et al., eds. The Dead Sea Scrolls of St. Mark's Monastery, Vol. I, The Isaiah Manuscript and the Habakkuk Commentary, and Vol. II, fasc. 2, "Plates and Transcription of the Manual of Discipline" (New Haven, American Schools of Oriental Research, 1950, 1951).

pended from the lines, rather than set upon them. Apart from a few tears and a dozen or so badly worn columns, the manuscript has been excellently preserved by the dry climate of the Dead Sea region and by the jar in which it was carefully sealed. The palaeography of the Isaiah scroll suggests that it was written during the second half of the second century B.C.; and this would make it the earliest manuscript of the group, and the oldest existing major manuscript of the Bible in any language. The text of the Isaiah manuscript differs notably in orthography and somewhat in morphology, but agrees to a remarkable degree with the Masoretic text, thus supporting the fidelity of the Masoretic tradition.[17]

The Manual of Discipline (1QS) is the next largest scroll in the group, with eleven columns of beautifully written Hebrew text that average twenty-six lines each. The five sheets of parchment, sewed together, form a scroll a little over six feet long and about nine inches high. It was brought to the American School in Jerusalem in two pieces, each tightly rolled and very brittle. The condition of the parchment is remarkably fine, without the signs of handling or wear evident in the Isaiah scroll. The scribe who copied the Manual document was obviously not the one who copied the Isaiah scroll, although the two copies are much the same. The style of writing indicates that 1QS was written a little later than the Isaiah scroll—perhaps between 100 and 75 B.C.[18]

The scroll with the most beautifully preserved writing is that of the Habakkuk Commentary [19] (1QpHab—"p" standing here for pesher, or commentary), a manuscript composed of two pieces

[17] M. Burrows, "Variant Readings in the Isaiah Manuscript," BASOR, No. 111 (1948), 16–24, and No. 113 (1949), 24–32.

[18] Among the numerous translations of the Manual, we note two: The Dead Sea Manual of Discipline, translation and notes by W. H. Brownlee (New Haven, American Schools of Oriental Research, 1951); and G. Lambert, "Le Manuel du Désert de Judée: Étude historique et traduction intégrale," NRT, LXXIII (1951), 938–975. A list of the translations may be found in W. H. Brownlee, "The Servant of the Lord in the Qumrân Scrolls," Pt. II, BASOR, No. 135, Oct., 1954, p. 33, n. 3. A complete summary of the contents of the Manual will be found in Chap. V, following.

[19] See p. 74 for a discussion of the term "commentary" as applied to this document.

sewed together, about five feet long and at present a little over five inches high, although originally it must have been about two inches higher, because several lines are missing from the bottom of each column. The script, different from that of 1QIsᵃ and 1QS, is remarkably clear, large, and regular, and the letters are hung from the lines as in the other scrolls. The most striking feature of this writer is his use of archaic Hebrew characters for the tetragrammaton in several places. The commentary deals with only the first two chapters of the Book of Habakkuk. This is of considerable interest, because the third chapter of the canonical book is a psalm which many critics have thought a later addition. It may be noted again, as in the case of 1QIsᵃ, that the Hebrew text of Habakkuk used by the commentator is very close to that of the Masoretic tradition. This document is exceedingly important because of the light it throws upon the exegetical principles of the Qumrān sect, and upon the history of the community. On the basis of palaeography and historical allusions, the Habukkuk Commentary is to be dated probably in the latter half of the first century B.C.[20]

The fourth scroll in this group from 1Q, because of its extremely brittle condition, has not yet been unrolled. However, several fragments have been removed, which reveal a neat and fine script. The language is Aramaic, and a few words that have been identified suggest that the scroll may be the long-lost Apocryphal Book of Lamech.[21]

The Scrolls Purchased by the Hebrew University

At the same time that the Metropolitan of the Syrian Orthodox Convent in Jerusalem was negotiating for the group of manuscripts just described, Professor Sukenik of the Hebrew University of

[20] See K. Elliger, *Studien zum Habakuk-Kommentar vom Toten Meer* (Tübingen, 1953), the first definitive work on any of the documents from 1Q. There are now about a dozen different translations of the Habakkuk Commentary. Cf. W. H. Brownlee, "The Jerusalem Habakkuk Scroll," *BASOR*, No. 112 (1948), 8–18.

[21] See J. C. Trever, "Identification of the Aramaic Fourth Scroll from 'Ain Feshka," *BASOR*, No. 115 (1949), 8–10.

Jerusalem received word of the phenomenal manuscript find near the Dead Sea. Through the aid of both Christians and Moslems, Professor Sukenik acquired a number of scrolls and fragments for the Museum of Antiquities of the Hebrew University in Jerusalem.[22]

The most important scrolls in this group are one containing a collection of Thanksgiving Hymns (1QH), a work entitled for the time being The War of the Children of Light against the Children of Darkness (1QM), and a rather fragmentary Isaiah Scroll (1QIs[b]). The script, homogeneous in the three documents, is similar to that of the latest of the manuscripts published by the American Schools of Oriental Research, and so may be dated in the latter part of the first century B.C., or even later.

1QH came into Sukenik's hands in three badly mutilated leaves of leather. The scroll must have been a little over six feet long and about thirteen inches high, with about thirty-nine lines of writing in each of the twelve columns. There are about thirty-five hymns, whole and fragmentary, closely similar in style to the Biblical Psalms, which are quoted profusely. They have the same spirit and flavor as the hymns in the early part of Luke's Gospel: the Magnificat, the Benedictus, and the Nunc Dimittis. Although the Qumrān hymns are filled with Biblical phrases and ideas, they have a distinct mood of their own. Their language, situation, and theology reflect a later time than the Old Testament period.

The War Scroll (1QM) is more than nine feet long, with nineteen columns of writing, each about seventeen lines long. Neither the name of the author nor the name of the work is preserved in the text, which deals with a war between the "children of light" and the "children of darkness" (expressions found in 1QS, I, 9–10). The "children of light" are the descendants of Levi, Judah, and Benjamin; the "children of darkness" on the other hand are the

---

[22] The two preliminary reports on this material are found in E. L. Sukenik, *Megilloth Genuzoth* (2 vols., Jerusalem, 1948, 1950). The final publication of this material has now appeared in E. L. Sukenik, *Osar Hammegilloth haggenuzoth* (Jerusalem, 1954). Quotations from these scrolls are taken from this later work.

Courtesy of the American Schools of Oriental Research

Col. VII of the Habakkuk Commentary (1QpHab)

"troops of Edom and Moab, and the children of Ammon, Philistia and the troops of the Kittim of Asshur" (the Seleucids). The holy war which ensues is described in great detail, with the battle formation of the Jews, their banners and weapons of war, and the trumpet calls used to direct the battle. The prayers of the priests for the warriors as they go into battle are given, and the hymn of thanksgiving after the victory has been won. Many of these ritualistic and military details are reminiscent of the wars the children of Israel fought in conquering Canaan. This manuscript no doubt describes the struggles of the Jewish armies with their enemies from the Maccabean period down to the time of the Roman domination after 63 B.C.

The third scroll discussed by Professor Sukenik contains the text of Isaiah. 1QIs^b is much more fragmentary than 1QIs^a, and lacks the following chapters: 1–9, 11, 12, 14, 15, 17, 18, 21, 24, 25, 27, 31–34, 36, and 42. The other chapters are represented by fragments varying from a few verses to almost the entire chapter. The palaeography and other signs indicate that 1QIs^b was written after 1QIs^a, probably in the latter half of the first century B.C. In morphology and orthography, 1QIs^b is closer than IQIs^a to the text of the Masoretic tradition.

Fragments of Daniel

According to Professor G. Ernest Wright, the Syrian Archbishop brought to America early in February, 1949, several fragments of the Book of Daniel discovered in Cave 1. He describes them as follows:

In the matted mass of leather fragments were three sections from Daniel in addition to several fragments from some other piece of Hebrew religious literature. Interestingly enough, the three fragments of Daniel are from two different scrolls. Two pieces are paleographically near the Isaiah scroll, while the other is very similar to the Habakkuk script. Two pieces are from the same column and contain portions of Daniel 3:23–30 in Aramaic, while the third fragment contains portions of two columns: Dan. 1:10–16 and Dan. 2:2–6 (including the point where the Aramaic part of Daniel begins). One of the pieces of the passage from Dan. 3:23–30 measures 4 by 4½ in., and its companion from the same column is 2½ in. square. Together they show that the column must have been almost 6 in. wide. The other fragment measures 5½ by 3 in., and the columns were apparently less than 4 in. wide. . . . The text is substantially the same as that of our current He-

brew Bibles (the Masoretic text). The chief differences, like those in
the Isaiah manuscript, have to do with the spelling of words.[23]

If the Book of Daniel was written around 165 B.C., and if the
script of two of these fragments is similar to that of the Isaiah
scroll, which is dated about 125 B.C., then we are less than a century from the original—which no one thought possible in Old
Testament studies.

The Exploration of the Region Around Qumrān

At the end of February, 1952, it became known that the Bedouins had discovered more manuscript material in the region of
Qumrān. After the École Biblique and the Palestine Museum had
purchased fragments from this lot, it was decided to send an expedition to explore the region thoroughly for manuscript fragments. Père de Vaux of the École Biblique, Professor W. L. Reed,
director of the American School of Oriental Research in Jerusalem,
and several assistants pitched camp at the foot of the cliffs at
Qumrān on March 10, 1952, and for three weeks thereafter investi-
gated every cave and crevice in the rocky escarpment that they
could enter. Their purpose was threefold: to find the cave where
the Bedouins had discovered the fragments that had been purchased; to determine the area inhabited by the sect; and to discover,
if possible, more manuscripts.[24]

Several small, mobile groups, composed of a member of the
expedition and three or four Bedouins, were organized to explore,
section by section, the rocky, steep area reaching from Hajar al-
Asbah south past Râs Feshka—about six miles. The difficult terrain made the work slow and arduous. Sometimes exposed sherds
led to a find, but more often discoveries came only after fallen
rocks were cleared away or trenches were dug into the crevices. Two

---

[23] G. E. Wright, "Archaeological News and Views," BA, XII (1949), 33.
[24] For two reports on this expedition, see R. de Vaux, "Eloration de la
région de Qumrân," RB, LX (1953), 540–561, and W. L. Reed, "The
Qumrân Caves Expedition of March, 1952," BASOR, No. 135, Oct., 1954,
8–13.

hundred and thirty unsuccessful soundings were made, and pottery and other objects were found in thirty-nine caves and crevices. In twenty-five the pottery was similar to that at Khirbet Qumrān and Cave 1. Cave 2 (2Q), where the Bedouins had found the fragments they had sold to the authorities in Jerusalem, was further explored; and a crew under the direction of Henri de Contenson discovered Cave 3 (3Q), which contained the copper scrolls.

Unfortunately, circumstances did not permit thorough exploration of the plateau between the cliffs and the Sea, where the Bedouins later discovered the most productive manuscript cave in the side of Wadi Qumrān (Cave 4, or 4Q), just a stone's throw from the Khirbeh. Fragment-bearing Caves 5 and 6 (5Q and 6Q) also were discovered later.

Location and Nature of the Cave Sites

Of the caves explored by this expedition only a few were large enough for habitation by members of the community. The rest were used for storage, as the pottery remains indicate. Some deep crevices in the cliffs also must have been living quarters, from the evidence of jugs and cooking pots and lamps; and in one of them several large forked timbers, which could have been used only for tent poles, were found under the rocks. The large natural caves have been used by Bedouin shepherds through the centuries, so that the archaeological evidence in them is very meager.

The pottery sherds from these caves and crevices are clearly related to those from Cave 1 and the Khirbeh. The great majority consists of fragments of tall storage jars and the lids—over a hundred jars and about seventy lids—like the sherds from Cave 1. Twenty other ceramic pieces and some lamps have been recovered, but no coins.

Cave 2 (2Q)

The Bedouins found here the manuscript fragments they sold to the authorities in Jerusalem. Cave 2, one of the largest in the vicinity of Qumrān, is a short distance to the south of Cave 1 and

consists of several chambers, in two levels. The Bedouins left behind only two small manuscript fragments. The untouched sherds
were of a dozen tall jars, one lid, and three bowls.

Among the Biblical fragments from this cave were several short
passages from Jeremiah and others from Exodus, Numbers, Deuteronomy, Psalms, and Ruth. A fragment of Leviticus in early Hebrew
script also was here. Père de Vaux, studying the Jeremiah fragments, found a text close to that of the Masoretic tradition,
and at variance with the text which is the basis of the Greek
version.

Among the numerous non-Biblical fragments was a small part
of the Book of Jubilees in Hebrew. Added to the similar fragment
from Cave 1, it suggests that the Book of Jubilees was important
in the life of the Qumrān community. It is estimated that about
forty non-Biblical works were hidden in this cave, besides the
Biblical texts.

Represented by about a dozen fragments, is an Aramaic document of a liturgical character, describing a ceremony which has to
do with the use of bread.

Cave 3 (3Q)

Cave 3 is a little more than a mile north of Cave 1. A severe
earthquake had obstructed the entrance with large rocks, making
exploration difficult. Some pottery was found inside, including a
lamp, and sherds of several jugs and about forty tall jars and twenty-
six covers.

The extremely small manuscript fragments found in Cave 3 have
suffered greatly from the ravages of time. Père de Vaux describes
one small Isaiah fragment which seems to be a kind of commentary. Parts of the first lines of Isaiah 1, and a few broken lines
which seem to be a commentary on the passage, are written in a
neat script. Apart from one slight variation in the spelling of the
name Isaiah, the few legible words of the Biblical passage agree with
the Masoretic text. The other fragments are of a dozen different
manuscripts. One of them includes the phrase "the angel of the

face," which occurs in Jub. 1:27, 29, and the Testaments of the Twelve Patriarchs, Judah 25:2.[25]

The most exciting find of the whole expedition came from this cave: two copper scrolls, lying one upon the other, against the wall of the cave near the entrance.

The Copper Scrolls

Certainly the most important discovery during the exploration just described was of the two copper scrolls, one on top of the other against the wall near the entrance of Cave 3. Collapse of the ceiling placed them in a kind of niche and thus preserved them from mutilation or destruction for many centuries. During this long period, however, the tightly rolled strips of metal became corroded; and it has been impossible to unroll them. If the current tests in American laboratories fail to make oxidized copper like that of these scrolls pliable again, they will have to be cut into strips and studied in sections. In the meantime, the two scrolls lie in a showcase of the Palestine Museum in Jerusalem.

Père de Vaux has made two initial reports on this spectacular find, and Professor Kuhn has made as thorough a study as possible of the scrolls in their present condition. The following description is based on their accounts [26] and my own observations.

Originally the scrolls were three strips of copper, riveted together to form one sheet about 95 inches long. Two of the strips still remain together and, tightly rolled up, form the larger scroll found in the cave. The smaller scroll, found under the large one, is of course the third strip rolled up in the same way. That the two scrolls were originally attached is proved by the fact that the smaller one ([b]) has holes at the open end which correspond with rivets, spaced at identical intervals in the open end of the larger one ([a]). They were no doubt detached so that the roll would not be too bulky. When the long strips were rolled up the script, which was

---

[25] The phrase is derived from Is. 63:9.
[26] R. de Vaux, "Fouille au Khirbet Qumrân," *RB*, LX (1953), 84–85, and "Exploration de la région de Qumrân," *ibid.*, 540–561; K. G. Kuhn, "Les Rouleaux de cuivre de Qumran," *RB*, LXI (1954), 193–205.

beaten into the metal, faced the inside; but the backs of the letters are visible on the outside of the scrolls in reverse order.

The text of the scrolls, in Hebrew characters, contains ten to twelve columns of sixteen or seventeen lines each. The four columns legible on the outside of the scrolls make clear that the text is not a Biblical one. There seems to be a preponderance of numerical words, as well as numerical signs. Phrases are repeated—like *ḥpwr 'mwt*, which Professor Kuhn translates "interred at so many cubits." Many lines are not filled out, and not a single name of a person has appeared. The probability is that the scroll is a list or catalogue of some kind.

It could hardly be the list of laws or regulations Père de Vaux has suggested, for attachment to a wall. The few legible words seem to rule out his suggestion, and the metal strips have no markings to indicate where they were fastened. (Could they not have been placed in a wooden frame, he asks, and the wooden frame attached to the wall?)

Professor Kuhn believes that these scrolls were made in imitation of the rolls of skin found at Qumrān and were purposely planted in the cave where they were found, a little more than a mile north of the community center. He suggests that the text contains a description of the main building, and that the oft repeated phrase may refer to the places where the valuables of the sect were hidden. All this was recorded in permanent form and hidden at the time of the Roman troubles (beginning in A.D. 66), so that members of the community, returning after any destruction or dispersal, might have the necessary information for rebuilding on the site and for restoration of the communal life.

Conclusions

All the pottery found in the caves and crevices in the vicinity of Qumrān is contemporaneous with the main period of occupation—about 110 B.C. to A.D. 68. It is now clear that the sect used the community center on the plateau for various communal activities but lived in the caves and crevices in the near-by cliffs.

The fact that coins have not been found in the scores of caves and crevices explored near Qumrān is remarkable, in view of the large number unearthed in the community center. The lack of coins in the caves where the members of the sect lived is probably to be explained by the fact that they held all goods in common and practiced the discipline of poverty. All money transactions, carried on by the administrative officer, were no doubt confined to the community center, where most of the coins have been discovered.

Cave 4 (4Q)

In August, 1952, the Bedouins came across another manuscript-bearing cave overlooked by the explorers, dug out of the marly terrace of the community center, only a stone's throw from the Khirbeh. Most of the fragments got into the hands of the Bedouins before their clandestine operations were stopped; but contributions from institutions all over the world have made it possible to purchase them box by box, and scholars now are studying them in the Palestine Museum in Jerusalem, and preparing them for future publication.

As soon as word of this fabulous discovery was received, the Department of Antiquities halted the work of the Bedouins. With the aid of the École Biblique and the Palestine Museum it undertook a systematic excavation of the cave during the last week of September, 1952. A few more manuscript fragments and pottery remains were discovered, and a new opening in the plateau near by yielded some badly mutilated fragments. This is Cave 5 (5Q). The Bedouins found another hole in the rocks near the head of the wadi which contained some fragments and is known as Cave 6 (6Q). Among the fragments from 6Q is a passage from CDC which proves that this work was in the great library of the Qumrān community.

It will take time to assemble and publish this wealth of manuscript material. Arrangements have been made for the Oxford University Press to publish it under the direction of Père de Vaux. Until the *editio princeps* is published, however, fragments of unusual importance or of a representative character will be published from time to time, keeping the world of scholarship abreast of new developments.

The assembling of the fragments is done in a long room in the Palestine Museum where, on two long rows of tables, the fragments are placed between hundreds of glass plates as they are identified and fitted together. Professor Frank M. Cross, Jr., describes the preparation of the fragments from the time they enter the museum until they are placed between the glass plates:

The first steps in preparing the manuscripts are quite unexciting. The humidifier and the camel-hair brush are the chief pieces of equipment necessary, and patience the sole resource required of the scholar. Brittle, crinkled fragments are softened, and flattened between glass plates, first of all; then comes the delicate task of cleaning marly clay from the surface, and in some cases from the very pores of the leather or papyrus. Some of the fragments are extremely friable, so that to clean off the clay is to strip off the ink of the script as well. Others crumble at the touch of the brush unless backed with tape. Yet others have turned black in the process of time through the action of air and moisture. In the worst cases, a non-acid oil must be used to reveal the script on the deteriorated surface of the leather. Fortunately, the carbon ink used on the fragments responds well to infra-red rays; and fragments illegible to the naked eye are frequently decipherable on infra-red photographs.

After the tedious process of cleaning, the fragments are photographed and identified as to language and content (biblical, non-biblical, etc.). In the case of biblical material, identification proceeds easily. A word or two or even parts of words are sufficient to place it precisely; in the case of unknown works, identification proceeds more slowly, generally awaiting the collection of a number of fragments of the same work. In the case of non-canonical works, apocryphal, pseudepigraphical, and sectarian, known from ancient sources, or from recent discoveries, identification is complicated but fairly rapid. A concordance of the manuscripts from the first cave has been prepared, and a concordance of the Zadokite Fragments. Despite texts widely divergent from those preserved in translation, or in subsequent editions preserved until our day, the Intertestamental works soon reveal their identity by key words and characteristic phraseology. . . .

After identification of fragments, documents of the same order are placed on plates, and slowly manuscripts begin to collect until all fragments—ideally speaking—are identified and find their fellows.[27]

The finds from Cave 4 surpass the great discovery in 1947 in interest and importance. The list of works represented by these fragments is imposing. It includes every canonical book of the Old Testament with the possible exception of Esther. There are more manuscripts of Isaiah than of any other book of the Old Testament. After it come the Pentateuch, Psalms, Daniel, and Jeremiah. About a half a dozen books are represented by manuscripts written in the old Hebrew script. It is estimated that more than a hundred Biblical manuscripts may have been placed in this cave alone.

The importance of the manuscripts, however fragmentary, for the textual study of the Hebrew Old Testament cannot be over-estimated. Already publication of several fragments from Cave 4 has contributed to our knowledge of the Hebrew text. Here is a list of the published fragments with a brief summary of the conclusions:

1. F. M. Cross, Jr., "A New Qumran Biblical Fragment Related to the Original Hebrew Underlying the Septuagint," *BASOR*, No. 132, Dec., 1953, 8–26. It is clear that this fragment stands in the same general tradition as the Hebrew text which underlies the Septuagint. It therefore antedates the time of the standardization of the Hebrew textual tradition of Samuel.

2. J. Muilenburg, "A Qoheleth Scroll from Qumran," *BASOR*, No. 135, Oct., 1954, 20–28. This fragment shows that there was a Hebrew Book of Qoheleth by the middle of the second century B.C.

3. J. Muilenburg, "Fragments of Another Qumran Isaiah Scroll," *BASOR*, No. 135, Oct., 1954, 28–32. The text of these fragments conforms closely to the Masoretic text of our Hebrew Bibles.

4. P. W. Skehan, "A Fragment of the 'Song of Moses' (Deut.

[27] Cross, "The Manuscripts of the Dead Sea Caves," *BA*, XVII (1954), 15–16.

32) from Qumrān," *BASOR*, No. 136, Dec., 1954, 12–15. Like Professor Cross's Samuel fragment, this agrees with the Hebrew underlying the Septuagint translation.

There are also Hebrew and Aramaic fragments of several non-canonical works like Tobit, Jubilees, and the Enoch literature; and many more are sure to turn up. More than fifty Aramaic documents are represented among the fragments from Cave 4. The hundreds of fragments of unknown works which have already been cleaned and put under glass plates testify to the vast amount of literature from this intertestamental period which we do not know.

Sectarian works of the Qumrān community are also well represented among the Cave 4 fragments. There are paraphrases of several Biblical books, commentaries (*peshers*) on Isaiah, Malachi, and the Psalms, phylacteries,[28] liturgical texts establishing the Essene calendar, and a fragment with a cryptic script which Abbé Milik has deciphered. Of unique importance is a page of Biblical *Testimonia*, or manual of Biblical texts justifying the Messianic concepts of the community—among them, Deut. 18:18, 25–29, Num. 24:15–17, and Deut. 33:8–11. They deal with prophecies of the Prophet who is to come, of the Star which shall come out of Jacob, and regarding Levi. Several copies of the scrolls from Cave 1 appear in the fragments from Cave 4; also new texts of CDC.

Significance of the Qumrān Manuscripts

From these manuscripts we learn, first of all, of the life, practices, and teachings of a monastic community, probably Essene, which made its home in the vicinity of the Wadi Qumrān. The history of this sect as revealed by excavations of the site has already been discussed here, with several examples in which manuscripts and excavations have illustrated and corroborated each other.

Apart from a wealth of historical and theological material concerning the Qumrān sect, these manuscripts throw an extremely valuable light upon Old Testament studies. When all this material

---

[28] The Qumrān phylacteries differ from the one found at Murabba'at in that they contain the Ten Commandments.

becomes available to scholars it will greatly enrich our knowledge of Hebrew lexicography, grammar, and syntax.

The late dating of various books of the Old Testament must be given up now that manuscripts have been discovered which were used in the second century B.C. The *Hodayoth*, or Thanksgiving Psalms, which were composed not later than the second century B.C. and are full of quotations from the canonical Psalms, deal a death blow to the theory of many Old Testament scholars that some Psalms are of Maccabean origin. The numerous *peshers* by members of this community on such prophetical books as Habakkuk, Malachi, and Isaiah preclude Hellenistic elements in the canonical prophetical books, for which some scholars have argued.

The manuscripts from Qumrān will provide critics with a wealth of new texts to work on. Evidence is at hand which throws new light on the history of the Hebrew text, as well as on the Greek translation of the Old Testament. It has become certain that the standardization of the Hebrew text, basis of the Masoretic text of our Hebrew Bibles, began in the first century B.C. and was completed in Palestine before the Second Revolt. This, of course, pushes the sources of the Masoretic tradition back much farther than was supposed possible, and places the movement in Biblical interpretation associated with Aqiba at the end of the process of establishing an official text, instead of the beginning.

On the other hand, striking evidence shows that other recensions of the Hebrew text existed side by side with the "official" text, and enjoyed equal authority in their own localities or circles. This can be seen in the two Isaiah manuscripts from Cave 1. The text of 1QIs^b is closer to M than 1QIs^a. From all indications, 1QIs^b is younger than 1QIs^a; and it may be assumed that the scribes of the Qumrān sect replaced the older manuscript with a later one whose readings conformed to the official text which was the precursor of M. The additions and corrections in 1QIs^a, made by a later hand, agree with the official text, which was the common ancestor of 1QIs^b and M. According to the evidence of the Biblical fragments from Murabba'at, the official text had become firmly established by A.D. 135.

As we have noted, some Hebrew texts from Qumrān diverge radically from M, and follow generally the readings which underlie the Greek translation of the Old Testament. This suggests that divergences in the LXX are not due to mistranslations, theological interpretations, or expansions, but rather to a literal and faithful following by the Greek translators of a Hebrew text which itself had variant readings—indeed a revolutionary idea, which cannot be wholly accepted without fuller evidence.

A revival of interest in the Apocryphal and Pseudepigraphical works of the intertestamental period should grow out of the Qumrān discoveries. The number of such works in the library of the sect, known and unknown, is astounding, and so is the high esteem in which members of the community held them. Their love for the apocalyptic works, and for works which dealt with the calendar—Jubilees and the Enoch literature, for instance—justifies wonder as whether the cleavage between these books and the canonical books of the Hebrew Bible actually was as sharp as is usually imagined. Perhaps, as Baumgartner suggests, the broader Alexandrian canon was acceptable in the Bible of Jesus' time.[29] It is also hoped that this new material will throw light upon the original languages in which these intertestamental works were written, as well as upon the scope of "inter-Semitic" translations of them.

Perhaps most important of all is the significance of these manuscripts for New Testament studies.[30]

Palaeography has benefited tremendously from the discovery of the manuscripts in the desert sites. It is now possible to trace clearly the development of the various scripts used in the writing of these documents from the second century B.C. to the second century after Christ, and also to date with uncanny accuracy the various stages in their development. Our knowledge of the various

[29] W. Baumgartner, "Die Bedeutung der Höhlenfunde aus Palästina für die Theologie," STU, XXIV (1954), 49–63.
[30] See Chap. VIII, "The Qumrān Community and the New Testament."

scripts used in different kinds of documents has been greatly enlarged, especially by the material from Murabba'at. The fact that a number of fragments from several Biblical books found at Qumrān were written in archaic Hebrew shows that the scribes of this community were familiar with it and used it to a larger extent than has been realized.

Postscript

Since the summer of 1955, when this book was finished, it has been reported that the so-called "Lamech Scroll" from Cave 1 (see page 34) and the copper scroll from Cave 3 (see page 41) have been unrolled. According to an article in the New York *Times*, February 7, 1956, from Jerusalem, the "Lamech Scroll" has turned out to be an Aramaic version of Genesis with many stories and legends interwoven into the text. The copper scroll, according to a *Times* dispatch of January 12, 1956, was unrolled in Manchester, England, but its contents have not been divulged.

CHAPTER IV

Manuscript Discoveries at Khirbet Mird and Murabba'at

A T LEAST two more sites in the desert of Judea have yielded manuscript treasures to the tireless Bedouins of the Ta'amireh tribe. One is Khirbet al-Mird, a monastery ruin at the top of a conical peak more than a thousand feet high, about four miles northeast of the ancient Greek monastery of Mar Saba and nine miles southeast of Jerusalem. One can drive into the desert from Mar Saba by car within a half-hour's walk of the towering peak. From the Khirbeh on top, one has an awe-inspiring view of the rugged and desolate terrain to the Dead Sea a few miles eastward.

Here in solitary splendor once stood the great fortress Hyrcania, place of refuge for the Hasmonaean rulers.[1] Destroyed by Gabinius, a general under Pompey and proconsul of Syria in 57 B.C., it was rebuilt by Herod the Great and used as a secret prison for his special enemies.[2] Toward the end of the fifth century of the Christian Era, St. Sabas, the founder of Mar Saba, built a monastery on the ruins of the castle, and appropriately called it Kastellion. It was in use until the ninth century. Today only underground chambers, cisterns, beautiful mosaics covered with dirt, and broken-down walls are left.

[1] *AJ*, XIII, xvi, 3: "So Alexandra, not knowing what to do with any decency, committed the fortresses to them, all but Hyrcania and Alexandrium, and Marcherus, where her principal treasures were."
[2] *AJ*, XIV, v, 4; XV, x, 4.

Khirbet Mird attracted little attention through the centuries until recent times. Father Evaristus Mader, a Bavarian priest and Byzantine scholar of note, tells of making several discoveries in the ruins of the Kastellion during five different visits in the early part of this century.[3]

It was not until July, 1952, however, that the indefatigable Ta-'amireh discovered in an underground chamber of the ruined monastery a considerable number of Greek and Arabic documents, as well as several Christo-Palestinian Syriac fragments.[4] According to the first report of the find, the following fragments have been identified: Greek uncial fragments of codices of the Wisdom of Solomon, the Gospels of Mark and John, and the Acts of the Apostles, dating from the fifth to the eighth centuries, as well as some documents written in cursive style; Biblical fragments in Christo-Palestinian Syriac from Joshua, the Gospels of Matthew and Luke, the Acts of the Apostles, and the Epistle to the Colossians, as well as some non-literary papyri,[5] and Arabic papyri from the early Islamic period.

Between February and April, 1953, a Belgian archaeological expedition under Professor Robert de Langhe of the University of Louvain found more Greek, Syriac, and Arabic fragments at Khirbet Mird—among them, a passage from the *Andromache* of Euripides—confirming the discoveries of the Bedouins in the preceding year. The manuscript discoveries at Khirbet Mird of course have no relation to those at Qumrān, which are of a much earlier time.

Murabbaʻat

On June 30, 1954, I had the privilege of visiting the caves in Wadi Murabbaʻat which have produced some of the most sensa-

[3] Mader, "Conical Sundial and Ikon Inscription from the Kastellion Monastery on Khirbet el-Mird in the Wilderness of Juda," *JPOS*, IX (1929), 122–135.

[4] For early reports on this find, see R. de Vaux, "Fouille au Khirbet Qumrān," *RB*, LX (1953), 85, and Milik, *RB*, LX (1953), 526.

[5] Cf. the only published document so far from Khirbet Mird, J. T. Milik, "Une Inscription et une lettre en araméen Christo-palestinien," *RB*, LX (1953), 526–539. As Abbé Milik points out, these are the first Christo-Palestinian Syriac documents to be found in Palestine itself.

tional manuscript material in the entire desert region of Judea. These caves, in one of the most inaccessible regions of Palestine, have been hide-outs for fugitives of all sorts from the earliest times. To reach them one ordinarily makes a southeasterly trek from Bethlehem of six hours or more across the desert. It was my good fortune to reach Murabba'at by a much less strenuous route. By special arrangement of Brigadier-General Young, head of the defenses of Jerusalem, and Major Douglas, "admiral" of the Dead Sea Navy (a branch of the Arab Legion), a party of us set out on a small armed vessel for Wadi Daraja, about twelve miles south on the western shore of the Dead Sea. The wadi becomes known as Murabba'at a few miles to the west in the heart of the desert. After disembarking, we climbed the steep escarpment which forms the shore and headed into the desert. Within two hours we reached Murabba'at, where the almost vertical sides of the wadi plunge seven hundred feet to the dry river bed below. After sliding and rolling halfway down the northern side of the gorge, we finally came upon the caves.

Cave 1 is by far the largest, being about thirty feet high, fifteen feet wide, and one hundred and fifty feet long. At its entrance there is a vaulted cistern from the Roman period. Cave 2, immediately to the west, is a large chamber with shafts and galleries extending far back into the side of the ravine. Huge blocks of stone are still piled up inside it. Cave 3, some thirty feet farther to the west, is scarcely discernible in the rocky cliff. At the back of it is a narrow, vertical shaft seventy-five feet deep. It had nothing of archaeological value. Cave 4, a little higher on the side of the wadi and over three hundred feet farther west, has several communicating chambers and extends almost two hundred feet into the cliff.

From these tremendous caverns we looked out upon some of the wildest, most desolate scenery in the world. Hundreds of feet below, several rock-strewn wadi beds converged and made a tortuous way through the desert plateau to the Dead Sea beyond. All was quiet and lifeless, except for the pigeons we had disturbed in the caves.

© *Palestine Archaeological Museum*

A cistern at Qumrān with crack in the steps

NORTH
CLOISTER

© *Palestine Archaeological Museum*

The table and bench of the Qumrān Scriptorium exhibition at the
Palestine Archaeological Museum in Jerusalem (Jordan)

The Discovery of the Caves at Murabba 'at

The discovery of the caves at Murabba'at is as fantastic as the site itself, especially as Père de Vaux tells the story.[6] Toward the end of 1951 manuscript fragments from an unknown source began to reach Père de Vaux and Mr. Harding through various channels. After several false reports as to where they had been found Père de Vaux got into touch with the Ta'amireh Bedouins themselves. At first, the desert tribesmen were reluctant to reveal the source; but they finally let Mr. Harding and himself, together with a police escort—"in order to protect themselves from the jealousy of their fellow tribesmen"—accompany them to the site on January 21, 1952. The expedition was under the auspices of the Jordan Department of Antiquities, the French Archaeological School, and the Archaeological Museum of Palestine.

At Wadi Murabba'at, the party surprised Bedouins streaming out of the caves with their illicit booty. While the police were searching them the desert "cavemen" tried to slip their "hot" loot into the hands of Père de Vaux. As it turned out later, however, most of them had to be hired by the expedition for legitimate excavation, since the task was far greater than anyone had anticipated.

During the next six weeks the excavators encountered all sorts of difficulties. Supplies, brought across the desert on muleback, had to make the descent of the cliff on human backs. The only place where tents for the party could be erected was a narrow ledge in front of the two large caves. The floors of the caves were covered with a thick layer of fine dust which made breathing and seeing almost impossible when it was disturbed. With the cooperation of the Jordan Air Force, a generator was laboriously brought to the caves and set up, which made the work easier.

[6] For the preliminary report on this expedition, see R. de Vaux, "Les Grottes de Murabba'at et leurs documents," *RB*, LX (1953), 245–267. Cf. also F. M. Cross, Jr., "The Manuscripts of the Dead Sea Caves," *BA*, XVII (1954), 8–12.

The History of Occupation

The four caves discovered at Murabba'at were inhabited at various times from the Chalcolithic period (4000–3000 B.C.) down to Arab times (A.D. 1200–1400). The evidence indicates that Caves 1 and 2 were used much more than the others. Unfortunately the countless potsherds have been so damaged by falling rocks, successive occupations, and clandestine excavators that few can be reconstructed into ceramic forms. However, the aridity has preserved not only texts of unique importance but also remains not usually found at Palestinian sites, like fabrics, leather, basket work, and objects of wood.

Human occupation of the caves at Murabba'at seems to have begun with the Chalcolithic period, which is represented by strata in the four caves. The pottery found in this level is extremely fragmentary, but its type is clearly established by comparison with examples from similar strata at other Palestinian sites. Other small objects of flint and bone and fragments of basketwork have been unearthed in this level. The most interesting specimen is an adze with the wooden handle still intact and the leather thongs for tying the flint blade still present. All of these objects indicate that the caves at Murabba'at were inhabited during the Chalcolithic period by people who hunted, raised cattle, and cultivated the nearby plateau.

Among the few objects from the Middle Bronze Age (about 1900–1600 B.C.) found in the caves were a small alabaster vase and a Hyksos scarab. The occupation during this time must have been spotty and unimportant.

The same can be said for Iron Age II (900–600 B.C.) which is represented by a few potsherds, typical of the time and the place. Evidence of Iron Age occupation at Murabba'at brings to mind David's period of wandering in this general region as a fugitive. One recalls especially the incident described in the opening verses of I Sam. 24. David and Saul were playing hide-and-seek in the wilderness of Engedi (the Bible name of the desert region including Murabba'at). Saul, we are told, went into a cave "to relieve himself," evidently unaware that "David and his men were sitting in the innermost parts of the cave." David humiliated him by cutting off his skirt, but then allowed him to go on his way.

A puzzling point in this story is that David and his men could hide in a cave without being detected by Saul when he entered. Although David's "four hundred" followers may not all have been with him the cave must have been of considerable size to accommodate David and his bodyguard without their being seen. It is now clear that David and his men must have used a huge cavern like the ones at Murabba'at for hiding when they were being pursued by Saul.

Occupation of the caves at Murabba'at was especially intense during the first and second centuries of our era. The pottery from this period is abundant, but very fragmentary. Several tall jars that have been reconstructed are similar to those found at Qumrān.[7] Metal objects, which are numerous, include iron arrowheads, javelin tips, knives, a chisel, a sickle, needles, and nails. Many fabrics, pieces of leather, and fragments of basketware have been found. Most important are the twenty coins from this Roman occupation level. They date generally from the time of Nero to Hadrian and include nine from the time of the Second Jewish Revolt (A.D. 132–135). The numismatic evidence is in exact agreement, as we shall see, with the dating of the texts found in the caves.

A last period of occupation (thirteenth and fourteenth centuries) is confirmed by Arab coins, potsherds, and fragments of Arabic manuscripts.

After the caves were abandoned by man, they became frequented by wild beasts and pigeons. Père de Vaux tells us that the manure which had accumulated on the floor of the caverns for centuries was sold to the Jewish colonists in Bethlehem by the Ta'amireh tribesmen during the first years of the British Mandate. The Bedouins do not remember finding any manuscripts at that time, but

[7] Cf. RB, LX (1953), 97, 257.

it is quite possible that the orange groves around Bethlehem were fertilized with fragments of papyrus or skin from the caves.

The Texts

The most important discoveries at Murabba'at are the literary remains, in Hebrew, Aramaic, Greek, Latin, and Arabic.[8] Many manuscripts were torn to shreds, probably by the Roman soldiers who took this stronghold from the Jewish Zealots in the Second Revolt. Others were mutilated by the rats who lined their nests with scraps of manuscripts. Most of the material was found in Cave 2, but a few scraps of writing as well as a number of Hebrew ostraca were found in Cave 1. Caves 3 and 4 were entirely un-productive.

Probably the oldest document found at Murabba'at—certainly the most unusual—is a papyrus palimpsest, written in archaic Hebrew characters. The superimposed text is a list of Hebrew names with numerical signs. The scarcely legible writing under-neath seems to be a letter, although only a few words can be read. Père de Vaux believes this text is older than the Leviticus frag-ment in the same kind of script, that was found in Cave 1 at Qumrān. The writing on the Murabba'at palimpsest seems to ap-proximate closely that of the Lachish ostraca, which date from about 600 B.C.

About fifteen pieces of broken pottery, inscribed with Greek or Hebrew characters, were discovered in Cave 1 at Murabba'at. Most of these ostraca contain only a few letters, or a name at the most. However, one large fragment of a jar is inscribed with the first part of the Hebrew alphabet, each letter being written twice. On three different sherds a long Hebrew text of twelve incomplete lines was written.

Among the Greek documents on papyrus are two contracts con-cerned with marital affairs. One is dated in the seventh year of

---

[8] The following description is based on Père de Vaux's preliminary report on Murabba'at, in RB, LX (1953), 260–267.

Hadrian (A.D. 124). There are also an acknowledgment of a debt of the time of the consul Statilius Severus, A.D. 171, and two fragments of an unknown literary work. Other fragments on skin or parchment seem to be administrative documents, containing lists of Jewish names followed by numerical signs.

The only Latin document found at Murabba'at is so fragmentary that only a few words are legible. From the style of the minuscule writing, it may be dated no later than the second century.

There are also a number of fragments from Murabba'at in a cursive script that has not yet been satisfactorily deciphered.[9]

The Biblical texts, all from the first two centuries of our era, are few and badly mutilated. Their extremely fragmentary condition is probably due to intentional damage by the Roman soldiers who occupied the site after A.D. 135. These fragments include passages from Genesis, Exodus, Deuteronomy, and Isaiah. In addition, a complete phylactery was discovered, containing Exod. 13:1-10, 11-16, and Deut. 11:13-21, on a long, narrow strip of parchment, and the *Shema'* (Deut. 6:4-9) on another piece of the same parchment and in the same neat, minuscule writing.[10] These Biblical passages agree completely with the Masoretic tradition, even in spelling. An "open section," according to the Masoretic tradition, may even be observed in the text of the published fragment of Exodus. A comparison of these Murabba'at fragments with the Qumrān Biblical material reveals that the text of the Masoretic tradition was established some time between the First and the Second Jewish Revolt, i.e., between A.D. 68 and 135. No Apocryphal texts were discovered at Murabba'at.

By far the most interesting and important literary texts from Murabba'at are the Hebrew documents from the time of the Second Jewish Revolt against the Romans, A.D. 132-135. There are several Hebrew texts on papyrus which speak of "the deliverance of

---

[9] For an attempt at decipherment, see S. A. Birnbaum, "A Fragment in an Unknown Script," *PEQ*, LXXXIV (1952), 118-120, and "An Unknown Aramaic Cursive," *PEQ*, LXXXV (1953), 23-41.

[10] Of the fragments, Père de Vaux has published in *RB*, LX (1953), 268-269, one containing Exod. 6:7-9, as well as the *Shema'* of the phylactery.

Israel by the ministry of Simeon ben Kosiba, Prince of Israel." [11] Unquestionably this Simeon is the same figure Jewish sources refer to as Bar or Ben Koziba, and Christian works as Bar Kokhba, who directed the unsuccessful revolt against the Romans under Hadrian; and it is almost certain that we have here fragmentary copies of the proclamation of Jewish independence in A.D. 132. It is interesting that the texts from Murabba'at preserve the correct form of the name, Simeon ben Kosiba.[12]

In the same lot are two letters from Simeon ben Kosiba to Yeshua ben Galgola, one of his officers, who resided at Murabba'at. One of them has been published by Abbé Milik.[13] The correct restoration of the damaged signature is most certainly "Simeon ben Kosiba, Prince of Israel," which leaves little doubt as to the identity of the writer. The burden of the letter is the treatment of certain Galileans by Yeshua ben Galgola. If they were Christians, as Abbé Milik suggests, this is the earliest archaeological documentation of the presence of Christians in Palestine.[14]

Another letter in this lot, from two administrators of the village Beth Mashko to the same Yeshua ben Galgola, who is called the "head of the camp, or army," gives notice of the purchase of a cow and reports the approach of the Romans toward the village.[15]

These Hebrew documents from the period of the Second Jewish Revolt are truly sensational, the more so because of the meager

[11] Coins from the first year of the revolt bear the inscription "Simeon, Prince of Israel."

[12] Both Koziba ("liar") and Kokhba ("star") are obvious word-plays on the name. Cf. E. Schürer, *Geschichte des jüdischen Volkes im Zeitalter Jesu Christi*, 4th ed. (4 vols., Leipzig, 1901–1911), I, 682, n. 98.

[13] J. T. Milik, "Une Lettre de Siméon bar Kokheba," *RB*, LX (1953), 276–294.

[14] Among the numerous articles that have appeared in connection with this published document we note: H. L. Ginsberg, "Notes on the Two Published Letters to Jeshua ben Galgolah," *BASOR*, No. 131, Oct., 1953, 25–27; J. J. Rabinowitz, "Note sur la lettre de Bar Kokheba," *RB*, LXI (1954), 191–192; S. A. Birnbaum, "Bar Kokhba and Akiba," *PEQ*, LXXXVI (1954), 23–32.

[15] Published by Père de Vaux in "Quelques textes hébreux de Murabba'at," *RB*, LX (1953), 268–275. See further H. L. Ginsberg, *op. cit.*, and J. J. Rabinowitz, "A Hebrew Letter of the Second Century from Beth Mashko," *BASOR*, No. 131, Oct., 1953, 21–24.

literary sources of their period in Jewish history. Here are documents from Bar Kokhba himself, as well as from contemporaries
who lived and fought at his side in the unsuccessful attempt to
overthrow the Roman overlords. The very name, Simeon ben
Kosiba, has now been authenticated from contemporary sources.
We catch new glimpses of the administrative set-up of the Jewish
guerrilla forces under Simeon, and of the high cultural level of
common people who could write documents in a Hebrew heretofore associated with the Scribes and their schools.

Several paper fragments of Arabic texts, and a complete document on two sides of an oblong piece of paper, complete the discoveries at Murabba'at.

An Unknown Source of Manuscripts

In August, 1952, the Bedouins discovered another important
lot of manuscripts in three caves, the exact location of which has
not yet been determined.[16] Dates in the documents and coins
found with them make it certain that this cache, like the one at
Murabba'at, belonged to a group of Jewish revolutionaries of the
Second Revolt.

There are a few Biblical fragments in Hebrew from Genesis,
Numbers, and Psalms, and a complete phylactery like the one
from Murabba'at; also fragments of a parchment scroll containing
the Greek text of the Minor Prophets. Of the remaining parts of
Micah, Jonah, Nahum, Habakkuk, Zephaniah, and Zechariah,
Père Barthélemy has published a fragment from Micah (4:3–7).[17]
Among the startling conclusions that he reaches from his study
of this fragment are (1) that the Greek text is identical with the
common basic text of Aquila, Symmachus, and Theodotion, and
(2) it may well have been the same text as the Quinta of Origen.
Such assertions, of course, are still subject to doubt, until further
evidence is brought to light.

[16] Briefly described by Père de Vaux in "Fouille au Khirbet Qumrân," *RB*,
LX (1953), 85–86.
[17] D. Barthélemy, "Redécouverte d'un chaînon manquant de l'histoire de
la Septante," *RB*, LX (1953), 18–29.

Also in this group are a Hebrew letter to Simeon ben Kosiba, the leader of the Second Revolt; two contracts in Aramaic dated "third year of the liberation of Israel"; [18] several Greek and Aramaic documents from "the era of the province of Arabia," which would be after A.D. 106; and important Nabatean papyri in cursive script, most of them contracts. Abbé Starcky has published one of the contracts, which contains both Nabatean and Jewish names,[19] which shows that in the first century of the Christian Era Jews and Nabateans intermingled freely in the communities of southern Judea.

[18] See J. T. Milik: "Un Contrat juif de l'an 134 après J.-C.", RB, LXI (1954), 182–190.
[19] J. Starcky, "Un Contrat nabatéen sur papyrus," RB, LXI (1954), 161–181.

CHAPTER V

The Qumrān Community and the Manuscripts

W E HAVE seen the light that the excavations at Qumrān have thrown upon the history of the monastic sect which occupied the region for almost two hundred years. It now remains to study closely the organization, life, and teachings of the sect as revealed in the manuscripts found, and to determine its identity.

The document which describes the Qumrān community in greatest detail is the Manual of Discipline (1QS), discovered in Cave 1 in 1947.[1] Because the original name of the scroll is not known, the editors have given it the name Manual of Discipline, which aptly describes its contents. All references in this chapter will be to the Manual, unless otherwise noted.

The members of the community (*yaḥad*), both priests and laymen, were dedicated to a strict discipline under God. They were to seek God and His ordinances, and to do what was good and right before Him, as He had commanded His children through Moses and the prophets. They were to love everything which God had chosen, and to hate everything which He had rejected. They were to practice truth and righteousness and justice, and to walk no more in the stubbornness of a guilty heart and with lustful eyes (I, 1-7).

One of the most striking features of this sect is the idea of "com-

[1] See pp. 32–33. Fragments of copies of this scroll have been found in Cave 4.

munity" (*yaḥad,* or *koinonía*) which permeates every phase of life. "All the members shall be in true community and good humility and loyal love and zeal for righteousness, each toward his friend in the holy council and as sons of the holy conclave [*sōd*]" (II, 24–25). Not only in spiritual matters, but also in everyday living, the members of the sect were to practice community. "They shall eat together, i.e., communally, bless together and take counsel together" (VI, 2–3). "They shall also bring all their knowledge and their strength and their wealth into the community of God" (I, 11–12, to be compared with V, 2).[2] Their possessions were turned over to the "Supervisor of the property of the many" (VI, 19–20), and then became the property of the community. The deposits of neophytes, however, were kept separate and were not spent for the many, perhaps allowing for dismissal from the community at the end of their second year of probation.[3]

The Qumrān community was composed of both priests and laity: "At that time"—i.e., when the Community is set up according to the regulations in the Manual—"the men of the Community shall be set apart as a holy house for Aaron, to be united a holy of holies, and a house of community for Israel walking in perfection" (IX, 5–6, to be compared with V, 6, and VIII, 5–6). Here "Aaron" and "Israel" stand respectively for the priests and the laity.

The laity, which evidently included both women and children,[4] were divided into groups of thousands, hundreds, fifties, and tens, "according to the knowledge of each man of Israel" (II, 21–22), and the priests had authority over them in matters of law and property (IX, 7).

All members of the community, in democratic fashion, were allowed to vote on matters concerning Torah, property, or laws (V, 2–3). The assembly in which such matters were taken up is described in dramatic fashion: "This is the procedure for the

[2] Cf. the practice of the Essenes (*WJ,* II, viii, 3), and of the early Christian community (Acts 2:44 ff. and 4:32 ff.).

[3] Cf. CDC, XVIII, 1 ff., for a different regulation in regard to the sharing of wealth.

[4] See pp. 10–11.

session of the many, each in his assigned position: the priests shall sit down first, then the elders, second; then the rest of all the people shall sit down, each in his own place. And thus shall they be asked with regard to judgment, and to every counsel and matter which comes before the many, each answering his friend [or, presenting his knowledge] according to the counsel of the Community. Let not any one speak in the midst of the words of his neighbor, before his brother finishes speaking. And also let him not speak before his proper order, i.e., the one enrolled before him. The man who is asked, let him speak his part [or, in his turn], and in the session of the many let not any one speak anything which is not according to the pleasure of the many and the word [emending *Kî'* to *pî'*] of the man who is the Supervisor [*mebaqqer*] over the many. And every man who has anything to say to the many, who is not in the position of the man who asks the counsel of the Community, then he shall stand upon his feet and say, 'I have something to say to the many.' If they say to him [i.e., bid him], he shall speak" (VI, 8–13.) According to this description, the assembly is presided over by a Supervisor or Overseer (*paqīd*, according to VI, 14), and everyone has a chance to speak in his turn. But no one is to interrupt his brother while speaking.

Another group, the Council, which served as a kind of Supreme Court, is described in VIII, 1–4: "In the Council of the Community (there shall be) twelve men, (of whom) three are priests, perfect in all that is revealed of the whole Torah, to practise truth and righteousness and justice and loving devotion and to walk humbly each with his neighbor, to guard faithfulness in the land with a strong purpose and a broken spirit, and to expiate iniquity through deeds of justice and through the hardship of refining, and to walk with all in the measure of truth and in the proper reckoning of time." [5]

There were evidently organized cell groups of the Qumrān sect in every locality where ten men were members of the order: "And

---

[5] CDC, XI, 1 ff., describes a similar group of ten "judges," four from the tribes of Levi and Aaron, and six from Israel.

in every place where there are ten men of the Council of the
Community, there shall not cease from among them a man who is
a priest, and let each according to his rank sit before him and in
this way let them be asked for their counsel in respect to every
matter" (VI, 3–4).[6]

The members of the Qumrān sect were volunteers who agreed to
live by the regulations of the community. To become a member,
however, was difficult, as the rules of admission indicate. Anyone
of Israel who volunteered to join presented himself before the
Overseer of the community for examination as to his intelligence
and conduct. If he showed himself capable of living according to
the strict discipline of the sect, he was admitted "into the covenant
to turn to the truth and to turn away from all wickedness" (VI,
14–15).

After a period of unspecified length, the candidate appeared before the many and was examined "concerning his affairs, and as the
lot falls out according to the counsel of the many, he draws near
or draws apart" (VI, 16). If he qualified at this stage, he became
a member of the community, but was still under certain restric-
tions: "And when he draws near to the Council of the Community,
he must not touch the purity of the many until they examine him
as to his spirit and his deeds until a full year is completed by him,
and he shall not share in the wealth of the Community, and when
he has completed a year in the midst of the Community, the many
shall ask concerning his ways with reference to his understanding
and his deeds in Torah. And if the lot falls out to him to draw
near to the conclave of the Community according to the judgment of the priest and the majority of the men of the convenant
(he shall draw near)." (VI, 16–19.)

A candidate in his first year as a novitiate, therefore, was not
allowed to participate in the purificatory rites of the community;
nor did he come under the laws which regulated the communal
possession of goods. After this year, the many examined him again

---

[6] Josephus writes that the Essenes lived in every city (WJ, II, viii, 4).

and decided whether he was to go on. If he was permitted to advance, "then they shall bring his wealth and property to the man who is the Supervisor of the property of the many, and they shall be recorded to his account by his hand [lit.], but not for the many shall he bring it forth [i.e., spend it]. He shall not touch the drink of the many until he has completed a second year among the men of the Community" (VI, 19–21).

A candidate in his second year as a novitiate entered into the purificatory rites of the community, but was not allowed to partake of the communal meal. He now shared in the community of possessions, although his own property was separately recorded so that it could be returned to him if he left the group before becoming a full member.

"Upon the completion of his second year, he [the Supervisor] shall examine him according to the judgment of the many, and if the lot falls out to him to draw near to the Community, he shall enroll him in the order of his assigned position in the midst of his brethren for Torah, and for justice, and for purity, and to share his property" (VI, 21–22).

By passing this final examination the candidate became a full member of the sect, entering into all of its activities.

The initiation ceremony was an elaborate affair. When the priests and Levites blessed God for all His redemptive acts, those who were entering the covenant said after them, "Amen! Amen!" [7] Next came the confession (with Brownlee): "We have perverted ourselves, [we have transgressed, we have sinned], we have done wickedly, we [and our fathers] before us—because we have walked [contrary to] true [ordinances]. And [God] is righ[teous who has executed] His justice upon us and upon [our] fathers, but His gracious compassion He has dealt unto us from everlasting to everlasting."

After the confession, the priests bless the men of the covenant: "May He bless thee with all good, and keep thee from all evil, and

[7] This rite is described in I, 16, to II, 18.

illumine thy heart with lively prudence, and favor thee with eternal knowledge, and lift His merciful face toward you for eternal peace." [8]

Then followed a long list of curses which the Levites hurled against the men of Belial, the enemies of God's covenant people, and all said "Amen! Amen!" [9]

Another interesting ceremony described in the Manual is a yearly rite in which the whole community was reviewed like an army, and those who had been faithful were promoted, whereas those who had sinned were demoted.[10]

A long section of the Manual (VI, 24, to VII, 25) deals with the penalties to be meted out against those in the community who sinned against God, their neighbors, or themselves. The list of offenses is imposing, and reflects the strict moral code under which the members of the community lived. Permanent excommunication, which was the worst punishment and often ended in agonizing death from starvation, is mentioned in another passage (VIII, 20, to IX, 2).[11]

Communal Rites

The two principal rites of the Qumrān community were baptism and the communal meal. Excavation of the Khirbeh near the Wadi Qumrān has brought to light several large, well constructed reservoirs with stairs, and many smaller reservoirs no doubt used for ablutions. The Manual indirectly alludes to the purificatory rites, making very plain that it is not the water that makes a man spiritually pure: "He may not enter into the water to touch the purity of the holy men, for he will not be cleansed unless he has turned from his wickedness, for uncleanness is with all the transgressors of His word" (V, 13–14). And again, the sinner "cannot purify himself by atonement, he cannot cleanse himself with water

[8] The connection with Num. 6:24–26 is clear.
[9] Cf. Josephus, WJ, II, viii, 7, describing the initiatory rites of the Essenes.
[10] II, 19–23, and V, 21–24.
[11] Josephus, WJ, II, viii, 8, describes the horrible death which awaited those Essenes who had been excommunicated.

of impurity [i.e., water to take away impurity], nor sanctify himself with seas or rivers, nor can he cleanse himself with any water of washing. Unclean, unclean shall he be as long as he rejects the commandments of God without being instructed in the Community's counsel. For it is in the spirit of God's true counsel in regard to the ways of a man that all his iniquities will be atoned for so that he may look upon the light of life, and by a holy spirit for community in His truth he will be cleansed from all his iniquities and by an upright and humble spirit his sin shall be atoned for. And by the submission of his soul to all of God's ordinances his flesh will be cleansed, so that he may sprinkle himself with water of impurity and sanctify himself with rippling water." (III, 4-9.) Outward lustrations are no substitute for inward purity of heart. The Holy Spirit, and not water, cleanses a man of his iniquities. The outward washing with water is only a symbol of the inward cleansing of man's heart by the Spirit.[12]

Another important communal activity described in the Manual is partaking of the communal meal: "They shall eat communally, and bless communally, and take counsel communally" (VI, 2-3). "And it shall be when they arrange the table to eat, or the wine to drink, the priest shall stretch forth his hand first to bless with the first fruits of the bread and the wine" (VI, 4-5, omitting dittography in the original text). Further information about the communal meal is found in the unpublished columns of the Manual, where "the Messiah of Israel" is said to be present at the ritual meals. The quoted phrase suggests that these meals were considered to be Messianic meals, at which the Messiah was present. Their significance, in relation to the sacramental meal instituted by Jesus, is discussed in Chapter VIII, "The Qumrān Community and the New Testament." [13]

[12] Cf. CDC, XII, 1 ff., on purification with water: "As to being cleansed in water. No man shall wash in water that is filthy or insufficient for a man's bath. None shall cleanse himself in the waters of a vessel. And every pool in a rock in which there is not sufficient water for a bath, which an unclean person has touched, its waters shall be unclean like the waters of the vessel."

[13] Cf. also WJ, II, viii, 5, Josephus's detailed description of the communal meal of the Essenes.

Times and Seasons

Time, to the members of the Qumrān sect, was a sacred trust from God, and the times and seasons were opportunities to remember God and His goodness. Every member of the sect set his heart "to learn all the wisdom found with reference to the times, and to set apart the ordinance of the time" (IX, 13–14). Parts of the day and night were set apart for special prayers and meditation. "With the coming of day and night, I will enter into the covenant of God, and with the outgoing of evening and morning, I will recite His ordinances" (X, 10). The following passage (X, 1–3) expresses the same idea in a more lyrical way:

> During the periods, I shall chant the Ordinance:
> At the beginning of the dominion of light, with its circuit,
> And at its withdrawal to the habitation of its ordinance;
> In the beginning of the watches of darkness,
> When He opens their storehouse and places them on high;
> (And) in their circuit when they are withdrawn by reason of light.
> When the luminaries are rising from the abode of holiness
> And when they withdraw to the habitation of glory.[14]

Even throughout the long night members of the community studied the Torah in three shifts. "And let there not cease to be, where there are ten, a man who studies Torah day and night, continually, concerning the duties toward his neighbor. And let the many keep awake in the Community a third of all the nights of the year in order to read in the Book and to study the law and to bless in the Community." (VI, 6–8.) There was not a moment of the day or night that someone was not studying or reading the Word of God in the Qumrān community. And wherever there were ten members of the community, one man among them devoted himself exclusively to the study of Torah.[15]

[14] Rendering of A. Dupont-Sommer, *The Jewish Sect of Qumran and the Essenes*, p. 105.

[15] Cf. Josh. 1:18 and Ps. 1:2, where mention is made of meditating on the Law day and night.

This interest in the sacramental use of time was manifested also by the community's rigid calendar of sacred festivals and seasons. Several passages in the Manual demand strict adherence to the religious calendar of the sect: "And to walk before Him perfectly in all things which are revealed, according to their appointed seasons" (I, 8–9). "And not to transgress in any one of all the words of God in their periods, and not to advance their times, and not to lag behind in any of their seasons" (I, 13–15). "And he shall establish his steps to walk perfectly in all the ways of God, as He has commanded, in regard to His appointed seasons" (III, 9–10).

The seasons, times, and periods of the religious calendar of the Qumrān sect were appointed by God and especially revealed to them. Therefore they were under special obligation to observe them as God had ordained them.[16]

The community's religious calendar is described in a little poem in the Manual. It is difficult to translate in places, but the general meaning is clear. "At the entrance of seasons, at the days of a new moon together with their circuit, with their bonds one to another, in their being renewed and being great for the holy of holies and a sign 'n' "—an esoteric sign, or the first letter of an esoteric word, or simply a scribal omission [17]—"for the key of his eternal mercies in every period that will be. In the beginning of months for their seasons and holy days in their order for a memorial in their seasons. With an offering of lips I will bless Him, according to the ordinance engraved forever, at the beginning of years and in the circuit of their seasons when He fulfills the ordinance of their order on the appointed day of each of them: the season of reaping to the summer, and the season of sowing to the season of vegetation, the

---

[16] Cf. CDC, V, 1–2, VIII, 15, XX, 1. In V, 1–2, Israel is said to have erred in these matters. Therefore the true calendar was revealed to this Community of the New Covenant.

[17] Some of the textual problems and enigmas in 1QS will undoubtedly be cleared up when the copies of this text from Cave 4 are available for comparison.

season of years to their weeks, and the beginning of their weeks to a season of liberty" (X, 3–8).[18]

A careful study of this passage makes clear that the calendar of the Qumrān community was the same as the one described in the Book of Jubilees VI, 23 ff., and in the Book of Enoch, LXXII–LXXXIII. It is a calendar of 364 days, divided into four seasons of three months each, or thirteen weeks to a season. As a solar calendar it differed from the lunar calendar of Rabbinic Judaism, which was divided into thirteen months of twenty-eight days each. The fact, among others, that fragments of both Jubilees and Enoch have been found in the Qumrān caves shows that these works may have been composed by members of this sect, or their spiritual forebears, the Hasidim.

Teachings

The *Weltanschauung* of the Qumrān sect is set forth in a long, carefully composed section of the Manual, which seems to be a distinct unit by itself (III, 13, to IV, 26). It was written "for the wise men, to instruct and teach all the sons of light in the generations of all mankind." After a few introductory words about the creative and sustaining power of God, the writer begins the main argument of the section: "And He set for man two spirits, by which to walk until the season of His visitation. They are the spirits of truth and perversion. In a spring of light is the source of truth, and from a fountain of darkness is the source of perversion. In the hand of the prince of light is the rule over all the sons of righteousness; in the ways of light they walk. But in the hand of the angel of darkness is all the rule over the sons of perversion; and in the ways of darkness they walk."

It is because of the angel of darkness that the righteous go astray, but "the God of Israel and His angel of truth help all the sons of light."

"And He has created the spirits of light and darkness and upon

[18] "Season of liberty" obviously refers to the year of Jubilees as described in Lev. 25:8 ff.

them He has established all His works. . . . One of them God has loved for all the duration of the ages, and in all its deeds He delights forever. As for the other, He has despised its counsel, and all its ways He hates forever."

Then follows a lengthy description of the ways of these two spirits. They are in a titanic struggle, which ends only when God destroys evil. In these two spirits "are the generations of all men (divided), and in their divisions all their armies receive an inheritance, and in their ways do they walk. . . . But God, through the mysteries of His understanding and His glorious wisdom, has appointed an end for the existence of perversity, and at the appointed time of the visitation He will destroy it forever. And then truth shall emerge forever on the earth."

According to this most significant document, man's soul was endowed by the Creator with two spirits, good and bad, which struggle continually for supremacy over his life. The dualism in man corresponds to a dualism inherent in the universe, as represented by the Prince of Light and the Prince of Darkness, sometimes referred to as Belial in the sectarian documents. They and their armies are in continual battle until God, at His appointed time, will destroy the forces of darkness and establish His truth forever.

This dualistic view of the universe is even more clearly expressed in another document found in Cave 1 in 1947, called The War of the Children of Light Against the Children of Darkness (1QM). Here the children of light (representing the Jews of the tribes of Levi, Judah and Benjamin) are described as being in conflict with the children of darkness (representing the traditional enemies of God's people—the Edomites, Moabites, Ammonites, Philistines, and the Kittim of Assyria, or the Seleucids). The army of the children of light is arranged in groups of thousands, hundreds, fifties, and tens. They fight according to instructions which are more theological than military. The banners they carry are inscribed with pious mottoes. On the great ensign at the head of the army is inscribed, "Army of God"; and the banners at the head of the various groups read, "Wrath of God, full of anger, against Belial and all the people of his party, without any survivors," "From God comes the force of battle against all sinful flesh," "Thanks to the power of God the position of the wicked has yielded," and "Praises to God on the harp." The priests and Levites give appropriate signals on trumpets and horns, reminiscent of the musical blasts that shattered the walls of Jericho. The battle itself is liturgically surrounded by prayers and hymns uttered by the priests. Before the battle, the chief priest addresses words of encouragement to the troops, and then hurls curses against the enemy. After the battle, all bless the name of the God of Israel who has given them the victory.

Of course, it is not an ordinary battle that is described. It no doubt has its setting in the many battles of the Jews against their earthly enemies, especially during the Maccabean struggle. But this is really a battle of cosmic significance, a holy war in which the forces of darkness are lined up against the army of light. The evil host is completely destroyed, and the victorious saints, in strict battle array, sing an anthem of praise to their Deliverer.

The dualism so clearly expressed in both 1QS and 1QM is reflected in other works of the intertestamental period, like Jubilees, Enoch, and the Testaments of the Twelve Patriarchs. The last of these specifically mentions the doctrine of the Two Ways and of the Two Spirits in the following passages (Asher 1:3–5 and Judah 20:1): "Two ways hath God given to the sons of men, and two inclinations and two kinds of action and two modes and two issues. Therefore are all things by twos, one over against the other. For there are two ways of good and evil, and with these are the two inclinations in our breasts discriminating them." "Know, therefore, my children, that two spirits wait upon man—the spirit of truth and the spirit of deceit." [19]

The origin of the dualistic system set forth in the Manual is

[19] Cf. also the little tract on the "Two Ways" which became incorporated in early Christian works like the Letter of Barnabas and the Didachē. Its Jewish background is now clear.

probably to be found in Iranian thought, which conceives of the world as torn between the two opposing forces of good and evil, light and darkness, represented by Spenta Mainyu (Holy Spirit) and Anra Mainyu (Evil Spirit). But in Judaism this dualism is set in the context of the one, true and living God, who creates the spirits of light and darkness (III, 25), and who has complete control of the conflict and its ultimate outcome.[20]

The members of the Qumrān community lived pure and holy lives in strict accord with the highest ethical standards. Negatively, they were to keep away from evil associates and sin of every form. Positively, they were "to practice truth, unity and humility, righteousness and justice, and loving devotion, and humbly to walk in all their ways" (V, 3–4), which was the noblest description of an upright man that the Old Testament prophets had given.[21] If members of the community broke any of the rules of conduct penalties ranging from reduction of food allowances to suspension, and even expulsion from the group, were imposed (VI, 1, to VII, 25).

"Knowledge" and "prudence" are prominent words in the sectarian documents. Knowledge belongs to God, and by knowledge He brought everything into being (XI, 11). God is the source of knowledge (XI, 3, 18). To the upright He gives insight into His knowledge (IV, 22). The writer of the closing hymn of the Manual says that he has beheld the divine wisdom which is withheld from men of knowledge (XI, 6), therefore he can sing with knowledge (X, 9).

When the priest blessed those who entered into the covenant, he asked that God might illumine their hearts with "lively prudence," and favor them with eternal knowledge (II, 3). Not only were the members of the community to be strictly examined in regard to their prudence (V, 21, 23, etc.), but they were also to learn prudence (IX, 13). For the Qumrān sect, therefore, true wisdom came

---

[20] On the relation of the dualism of the Qumrān sect and Zoroastrianism, see K. G. Kuhn, "Die Sektenschrift und die iranische Religion," ZTK, XLIX (1952), 245–260; also A. Dupont-Sommer, op. cit., 118–130.

[21] Cf. Mic. 6:8.

from God. It was the unveiling of the mysteries of truth to those who lived in the covenant community.[22]

As has already been noted, every book of the Old Testament canon, with the possible exception of Esther, was represented by manuscript material in the caves at Qumrān; and numerous commentaries on various books of the Old Testament have been found there. Both the books of Moses and those of the prophets were studied day and night in order to understand the true meaning of these works. Members of the community at Qumrān were steeped in the Scriptures, for there they learned how God wanted them to live, and what He had in mind for the future.

The Habakkuk Commentary states that God "has made known all the mysteries of the words of His servants the prophets" to the Teacher of Righteousness (VII, 3–5). In other words, the interpretation of Scripture was in the hands of the leader of the community, who had special insight into its meaning. Fortunately, 1QpHab is a clear example of how an Old Testament book was interpreted by the community. It is not a commentary in the technical sense, because it does not deal with philological problems or historical matters. The writer simply applies the message of the book, i.e., its scenes, events, and teachings, to his own time, thus bringing out the hidden meaning of the original text. In this sense 1QpHab is more accurately a midrash.[23]

Perhaps the most unique aspect of the Qumrān sect is its eschatological character. These covenanters believed that they were the true Israel, and that through them the Messiah from Aaron and Israel would come. They were chosen by God to make atone-

---

[22] That there are Gnostic elements in the sectarian documents of Qumrān cannot be denied; but one would hardly call this a Gnostic sect. Prof. Marcus characterizes the Essenes and the Qumrān-Damascus covenanters as gnosticizing Pharisees, further specifying that they were probably more gnostic than most apocalyptic Pharisees but less gnostic than those Jews regarded by the Tannaite authorities as heretics and referred to by them as *Minim* (R. Marcus, "Pharisees, Essenes and Gnostics," *JBL*, LXXIII [1954], 161). See also I. Sonne, "A Hymn Against Heretics in the Newly Discovered Scrolls," *HUCA*, XXXIII, Pt. 1 (1950–51), 275–313.

[23] Cf. W. H. Brownlee, "Biblical Interpretation Among the Sectaries of the Dead Sea Scrolls," *BA*, XIV (1951), 54–76.

ment for the whole earth and thus bring perversity to an end. The Messianic character of their communal meals and the apocalyptic character of 1QM emphasize this aspect of the community's teachings. They believed that they were living in the last days, when the kingdom of Belial was about to be destroyed and God's kingdom of righteousness and truth would be set up.[24]

In conclusion, then, we may say that the Qumrān sect was a monastic community whose members practiced the common life according to strict regulations; it was a covenant community which lived according to the requirements of the New Covenant; it was a sacramental community in that every phase of life was lived in accordance with the divine ordinances; it was a priestly community in that its life was directed by the priests, or sons of Zadok; it was a Bible-centered community, where the Scriptures were read and studied day and night, and where Biblical texts were continually copied by members of the group; and finally, it was an apocalyptic community, waiting expectantly for the quick overthrow of evil and the establishment of God's kingdom here on earth.

[24] See especially W. H. Brownlee, "The Servant of the Lord in the Qumrān Scrolls," *BASOR*, No. 132, Dec., 1953, 8–15, and No. 135, Oct., 1954, 33–38.

CHAPTER VI

The Qumrān Community and the Damascus Sect

I N 1896 two groups of Hebrew manuscripts were discovered in the genizah of a medieval synagogue at Cairo. They tell of the "sons of Zadok," Jews who migrated to Damascus and, under the leadership of the "Star," organized the Party of the New Covenant—sometimes called the Damascus sect, or the Covenanters of Damascus. Solomon Schechter published the documents in 1910,[1] and several further editions of the text, with translations and commentaries, have appeared since then.[2]

In general, this Zadokite Work (CDC) may be divided into two parts: (1) the origin and migration of the Covenanters (chaps. I–IX); and (2) the laws of the Covenanters (chaps. X–XX). It was written in almost pure Biblical Hebrew, enriched by a few Aramaisms and a few Mishnaic and Talmudic expressions.

Since the discovery of the Qumrān manuscripts in 1947, the

---

[1] S. Schechter, ed., *Documents of Jewish Sectaries* (2 vols., New York, 1910), Vol. I, *Fragments of a Zadokite Work*. See also R. H. Charles et al., eds., *The Apocrypha and Pseudepigrapha of the Old Testament in English* (2 vols., Oxford, 1913), in which "Fragments of a Zadokite Work" appears on pp. 785–834 of Vol. II. The citations here are from the Charles edition.

[2] H. H. Hvidberg, *Menigheden af den nye Pagt i Damascus* (Copenhagen, 1928), with a good survey of literature on the subject. L. Rost, *Die Damaskusschrift* (Kleine Texte für Vorlesungen und Uebungen, No. 167, Berlin, 1933), with a good bibliography. S. Zeitlin, *The Zadokite Fragments* (JQR Monograph Series, No. 1, Philadelphia, 1952). C. Rabin, ed. and transl., *The Zadokite Documents* (Oxford, 1954).

close affinities of CDC to this new material, especially 1QS and 1QpHab, have become increasingly clear. There are striking resemblances not only in style and terminology of the writing but also in the organization and structure of both the Damascus sect and the Qumrān community which the documents describe.

1QpHab and CDC, for instance, have the following phrases in common: "teacher of righteousness," "man of lies," "oracle of lies," "New Covenant," "period of wickedness." Almost every line of 1QS contains words and phrases reminiscent of CDC. Some important terms used in both documents are "to enter the covenant," "Belial," "Supervisor" (*mebaqqer*), "order" (*serek*), "period of time" (*qēṣ*), the "many," "stubbornness of heart," and "sons of Zadok." As Professor Brownlee writes, "there is such a common fund of language and ideas between the Dead Sea Scrolls and the Damascus Document (CDC) that on that ground alone there is no possibility of doubt as to the near kinship, if not absolute identity, of their respective sects." [3]

More important than affinity of ideas and words is the close literary relationship between CDC and 1QS, which the following parallel passages make clear:

CDC, III, 1–2: "And to choose what he approveth, and to reject what he hateth; to walk uprightly in all his ways, and not to go about in the thoughts of an evil imagination and (with) eyes (full) of fornication."

1QS, I, 3–4, 6: "And to love everything that He chooses, and to hate all that He despises. . . . And not to walk any more in the stubbornness of an evil heart and (with) eyes (full) of fornication."

CDC, IX, 50–53: "But all they who hold fast by these judgments in going out and coming in according to the Law, and listen to the voice of the Teacher and confess before God (saying) 'We have done wickedly, we and our fathers, because we have walked

[3] W. H. Brownlee, "A Comparison of the Covenanters of the Dead Sea Scrolls with Pre-Christian Jewish Sects," *BA*, XIII (1950), 51.

contrary to the statutes of the covenant, and true is thy judgment against us,' and (who) lift not the hand against his holy statutes, his righteous judgment, and the testimony of his truth; and are chastised by the first judgments with which the children of the men of the Community [with slight emendation] were judged."

1QS, I, 24–26: "[Then all] who enter into the covenant shall confess after them, saying, 'We have perverted ourselves, [we have transgressed, we have sinned], we have done wickedly, we [and our fathers] before us—because we have walked [contrary to] true [ordinances]. And [God] is righ[teous who has executed] his justice upon us and upon [our] fathers." (Brownlee's translation.)

1QS, IX, 10: "But they shall be judged by the first judgments with which the men of the Community began to be chastised."

CDC, XVII, 2: "They shall be numbered by all their names, the priests first, the Levites second, the children of Israel third, and the proselyte fourth."

1QS, II, 20–21: "The priests shall enter the covenant first . . . and after them the Levites shall enter, then thirdly, all the people."

CDC, XV, 4, 2: "Until there arises the Messiah from Aaron and Israel; and these statutes are to give instruction so that the whole nation may walk in them according to the Law always."

1QS, IX, 11–12: "Until the coming of a Prophet and the anointed ones of Aaron and Israel. These are the ordinances in which the wise man is to walk with every living being, according to the proper reckoning of every time."

CDC, XV, 5: "And when there arise ten, the man who is a priest . . . shall not depart."

1QS, VI, 3–4: "And in every place where there are ten men . . . there shall not cease from among them a man who is priest."

CDC, X, 5, 2: "Thou shalt surely rebuke thy neighbor and not bear sin because of him. Every man . . . who brings a charge against his neighbor whom he had not rebuked before witnesses."

1QS, V, 26, to VI, 1: "Though he shall reprove him on the very day so as not to incur guilt because of him. And also let not a man bring accusation against his neighbor in the presence of the many who has not been subject to (previous) reproof before witnesses."

These parallel passages—and other shorter verbal parallels which are not quoted—leave little doubt that there is a literary relationship between these two documents. It is not easy to determine which is the source. Nevertheless, certain differences in terminology and ideas seem to indicate that CDC represents a later period.[4] If, of course, the Damascus migration, mentioned in CDC, corresponds to the break in the occupation of the Qumrān site during the reign of Herod the Great, then CDC could not have been written before the first century of the Christian Era. On the other hand, a fragment of CDC has been found in the caves at Qumrān, so that it must have been written before the fall of the community in A.D. 68.

A comparison of CDC with the Qumrān documents, especially 1QS, will disclose very quickly the similarities as well as differences in structure and organization between the Damascus Covenanters and the Qumrān community. In both CDC (VI, 2) and 1QS (V, 2, 9) "sons of Zadok" designates the members of the sect.[5] They are the Party of the New Covenant, separated from Israel to safeguard the true doctrine imparted to them by God. (CDC, VIII, 15, IX, 28, 37; 1QpHab, II, 3. 1QS, V, 8, speaks about entering into the covenant of God, but the term "New Covenant" is not found in 1QS in connection with the community.)

According to CDC, the Covenanters were divided into four groups: priests; Levites; the people; and the proselytes. In this order they were to be seated at the meetings of the sect (CDC, XVII, 2–3). In the Qumrān community there seem to have been only three groups, seated in the following order at the sessions of the many: priests; Levites; and the people (1QS, II, 21–22, VI,

[4] M. Burrows, "The Discipline Manual of the Judaean Covenanters," OS, VIII (1950), 184.
[5] In 1QS the term designates the priests alone; in CDC it seems to include the whole sect.

8–9). The encampments (a word peculiar to CDC), or congrega-
tions, of the Damascus Covenanters must have varied widely in the
number of members, because they were divided according to thousands, hundreds, fifties, and tens (CDC, XV, 4). This same divi-
sion of membership prevailed in the Qumrān sect (1QS, II,
21–22). In CDC, XV, 5, we read: "And when there arise ten, the
man who is a priest learned in the Book of Hagu shall not depart."[6]
In almost every village, therefore, there must have been these cell-
groups of Covenanters, led by a priest, who was well versed in the
Book of Hagu.

What the Book of Hagu was is not clear. CDC, XI, 2, states that
the judges of the congregation should be "learned in the Book of
Hagu and in the ordinances of the covenant." Until the time of
the Qumrān manuscript discoveries, these were the only known
references to this book. Now, however, in the unpublished column
of the Manual, found in the fragments from Cave 1, appears
another reference to the Book of Hagu, stating that the members
of the sect are to be instructed in it from their youth. Therefore, it
must have been some kind of manual for the priests and laity of
the sect. As Dr. Schechter wrote in 1910: "This might suggest that
the Sect was in possession of some sort of manual containing the
tenets of the Sect, and perhaps also a regular set of rules of discipline for the initiation of novices and penitents."[7] There could
hardly be a clearer description of the Manual (1QS) from the
Qumrān caves than this. There is a strong possibility, therefore,
that 1QS is actually the Book of Hagu, and that the Book of
Hagu is the correct title of the Manual of Discipline.

The administrative officer of the Damascus Covenanters was the
mebaqqer, or Supervisor, whose duties are described in CDC,
XVI.[8] He enforced the laws of the Party (CDC, X, 10–13, XV,
7–8), and supervised the admission of new members (CDC, XVI,
5–6, XIX, 8–12). He handled the money affairs of the members,

[6] The same idea is expressed in 1QS, VI, 3.
[7] S. Schechter, *op. cit.*, I, xvi.
[8] This official was also found in the Qumrān community, where he had to
do mainly with the admission of new members (1QS, VI, 12 ff.).

receiving from everyone two days' wages a month to be distributed to the poor (CDC, XVI, 8, XVIII, 2 ff.).

The *mebaqqer* was also the spiritual adviser of the group. "He shall instruct the many in the works of God, and shall make them understand his wondrous mighty acts, and shall narrate before them the things of the world since its creation. And he shall have mercy upon them as a father upon his children, and shall forgive all that incurred guilt. As a shepherd with his flock he shall loose all the bonds of their knots . . . oppressed and crushed in his congregation." (CDC, XVI, 1–4.)

The founder of the Damascus Covenanters was a remarkable character whom God raised up "to lead them in the way of his heart" (CDC, I, 7). He is mentioned frequently in CDC and 1QpHab, but 1QS is strangely silent about him. He is usually called the Teacher of Righteousness; but he is also known as the Unique Teacher and, perhaps, the Messiah if the interpretation of certain passages is correct.[9] In establishing the Covenant community according to the Law of Moses, he was completing the work of Moses, started so many generations ago. In 1QpHab, the Teacher of Righteousness is called a priest (II, 8), and unto him had God made known "all the mysteries of the words of his servants, the prophets" (VII, 4–5). He came to a violent end at the hands of the Wicked Priest, who "swallowed him up in the vexation of his wrath." (1QpHab, XI, 4–5. Cf. also CDC, IX, 29 [B].) It was probably after the death of the Teacher of Righteousness that the community left Judea for Damascus, where, under the leadership of the Star, or Lawgiver, they entered into the New Covenant (CDC, IX, 8, VIII, 8, IX, 28). According to CDC, the "men of war" who "walked with the man of lies" were to be consumed forty years after the death of the Teacher of Righteousness (CDC, IX, 39 [B]). This evidently corresponds to the Day of Judgment and the ushering in of the Messianic Age.

There is little doubt that this important figure assumed Messianic significance in the minds of the Damascus Covenanters.

[9] See p. 82.

Several passages point to this conclusion. "That they should walk throughout the full period of the wickedness . . . until there arises the Teacher of Righteousness in the end of days" (CDC, VIII, 9–10). And in 1QpHab, VIII, 1–3, the writer comments upon Hab. 2:4, "Its meaning concerns all the doers of the law in the house of Judah whom God will deliver from the house of judgment for the sake of their labor and their faith in the Teacher of Righteousness." Salvation for the members of the Qumrān community came through faith in the person of the Teacher of Righteousness. Therefore, the Teacher of Righteousness, as the object of saving faith, must have been regarded as more than human.

In connection with the passage just quoted, that the Teacher of Righteousness was to come after the period of wickedness, it should be noted that in another passage in CDC the Messiah from Aaron and Israel is also prophesied as coming after the period of wickedness, which seems to equate rather clearly the Teacher of Righteousness with the Messiah, both of whom appear after a period of wickedness (CDC, XV, 4).

One difficult verse, however, seems to contradict this identification of the Teacher of Righteousness with the Messiah: "From the day when there was gathered in the Unique Teacher until there shall arise the Messiah from Aaron and from Israel" (CDC, IX, 29 [B]). Here it is said that the Messiah shall return after the death of the Unique Teacher, which seems to imply that the writer is thinking of two different individuals. Dupont-Sommer, however, believes that it can still be interpreted in such a way as to allow the identification of the Teacher and the Messiah: "When the death of the great righteous man is referred to, the author employs the expression 'Teacher of Righteousness,' which suits his earthly career better. When, on the other hand, the ultimate coming is referred to, he gives him the title of 'the Anointed,' since this coming is, as it were, the flowering of his Messianic character." [10]

It is futile to try to correlate the historical allusions in CDC with the historical setting of 1QpHab. According to CDC, a reli-

[10] A. Dupont-Sommer, *The Jewish Sect of Qumrân and the Essenes*, p. 55.

gious awakening occurred among the laity and priests ("Israel and Aaron") three hundred and ninety years after the Babylonian Exile —or 196 B.C., reckoning from 586 B.C. (CDC, I, 5). Then, after twenty years of groping, God raised up for them a Teacher of Righteousness, which would bring us down to 176 B.C. How long this Teacher lived, we are not told, but in CDC, IX, 39, we are told that there were to be forty years between the death of the Teacher and the annihilation of the "men of war."

It is probable that these figures, given in CDC, are symbolic rather than literal. The three hundred and ninety years, for instance, is obviously derived from Ezek. 4:5, and is therefore to be interpreted symbolically. Then, too, the twenty and forty years may simply mean that the period between the death of the Teacher of Righteousness and the coming of the Messiah will be twice as long as the period of groping, before God sent the Teacher to his people. At any rate, the writer of CDC is undoubtedly trying to show by this chronology that the early origins of the Damascus Covenanters are to be sought among the Hasidim of Maccabean times.

In the opinion of most scholars, the writer of 1QpHab is describing the period of Jewish history just before the capture of Jerusalem in 63 B.C. by the Romans. The struggle between the Teacher of Righteousness and the Wicked Priest, probably Alexander Jannaeus or Aristobulus II, ends in the death of the Teacher, and Jerusalem falls to the Roman legions (the Kittim).[11]

Even though it may be impossible to correlate the historical allusions in these two documents, it should be noted that both mention the Teacher of Righteousness as well as his enemy, the Wicked Priest, or Man of Lies. It seems then that these terms could be used to designate the representative of the true priesthood of the sect and the false priesthood of the Temple at any time between the Maccabean period and the fall of the Hasmonean

---

[11] Cf. W. H. Brownlee, "The Historical Allusions of the Dead Sea Habakkuk Midrash," BASOR, No. 126 (1952), 10-20, listing different theories of the historical background of 1QpHab.

dynasty. The two documents therefore describe the same basic struggle between the sect and the corrupt priesthood of Jerusalem, but probably refer to different phases of the struggle.

The entrance requirements of the Damascus sect were far less strict than those of the Qumrān community. Everyone who entered the sect had to be examined by the *mebaqqer* as to "his works, his understanding, his might, his strength, and his wealth" (CDC, XVI, 4). After taking the oath of the covenant, the candidate was enrolled by the Supervisor as a member of the sect (CDC, XIX, 8). From certain passages in CDC, it appears that celibacy was not required of those who entered the Order. "And if they settle in camps according to the order of the land and take wives and beget children, they shall walk according to the law, and according to the judgments of the ordinances according to the order of the law as He spake, 'between a man and his wife, and between a father and his son.'" (IX, 1[A]. Cf. also VII, 8–11.)

The regulations regarding the community of goods were far less rigid than those of the Qumrān community, for the Damascus Covenanters had to give only two days' wages out of each month to the Supervisor for a community fund, which was used to "strengthen the hand of the poor and the needy. And to the aged man who . . . to the vagrant and him who was taken captive of a strange people. And to the virgin who . . . no man careth for" (CDC, XVIII, 2–5). There is no mention in CDC of the communal meal, which figures prominently in 1QS. This, of course, may be due to the fragmentary nature of the text.

The Damascus Covenanters seem to have had closer connections than the priesthood of the Qumrān sect with the Temple in Jerusalem. According to CDC, the Damascus Party considered the Temple at Jerusalem to be their Sanctuary, and Jerusalem to be their Holy City (XIII, 27, and IX, 46). But the priests were not allowed to share in the Temple ritual except under their own strict regulations (VIII, 11 ff).

A detailed description of the laws of the Covenanters, recorded in the second part of CDC (X–XX), is unnecessary here. Some general observations, however, may be in order. The Covenanters believed that God had revealed unto them the correct observances of times and seasons, which had been hidden from Israel. "But with them that held fast by the commandments of God (who were left of them), God confirmed the covenant of Israel forever, revealing unto them the hidden things wherein all Israel had erred: his holy sabbaths and his glorious festivals, his righteous testimonies and his true ways, and the desires of his will (the which if a man do, he shall live by them) he opened before them" (CDC, V, 1–2). This reminds us of the emphasis on the calendar in 1QS [12] and in the Book of Jubilees. In fact, CDC, XX, 1, may actually refer to the latter: "And as for the exact statement of their periods to put Israel in remembrance in regard to all these, behold, it is treated accurately in the Book of the Divisions of the Seasons according to their Jubilees and their Weeks." [13] Thus CDC can be added to the cycle of works—1QS, Jubilees, Enoch—which advocate the religious calendar revealed by God to His chosen ones.

The laws regarding the Sabbath (CDC, XIII, 1–27), dietary matters, and marriage (CDC, VII, 1–4, 9–11), which are stricter than those of orthodox Judaism, seem to have been directed particularly against the Pharisees.[14] Then too, the loyalty of the sect to the Prophets, and its recognition of books like Jubilees and other Pseudepigrapha as authoritative writings, set it off from the normative Judaism of their day, represented by the Pharisees.

A comparison of the organization and teachings of the Damascus Party of the New Covenant with those of the Qumrān sect reveals that the two groups were closely related, if not identical. Because of certain differences, however, which have been pointed out, it might be more accurate to say that the two groups described in CDC and 1QS represent different stages in the development of the sect. Which one of them is the earlier, and which one is the later, is still a matter for discussion. From the evidence at hand,

[12] See pp. 68–70.
[13] Cf. also CDC, XI, 4, which quotes Jub. 23:9.
[14] See S. Schechter, *op. cit.*, I, xvi–xviii, for the legal differences between the Damascus sect and the Pharisees.

it appears that CDC represents a later stage in the development of the community than 1 QS. Judgment will have to be withheld, however, until the material from Qumrān has been fully published and studied.

The fact that the Damascus Covenanters and the Qumrān community were closely related or identical groups raises an interesting problem as to the relation of the Qumrān sect with the Karaites, a Jewish sect which originated in the eighth century. Ever since the publication of CDC in 1910, scholars have noted that its teachings closely resembled those of the Karaites.[15]

It has also been frequently pointed out that Kirkisānī, a Karaite scholar of the tenth century after Christ, probably referred to CDC, or a work like it, in his *Book of Lights and Watch-Towers*:

After the Rabbanites appeared the Sadducees; their leaders were Zadok and Boethus. They were, according to the Rabbanites, pupils of Antigonus who succeeded Simeon the Righteous and received instruction from him. Zadok was the first who exposed the Rabbanites and disagreed with them; he discovered part of the truth and wrote books in which he strongly rebuked and attacked them. He did not adduce any proofs for anything he said, but limited himself to mere statements; excepting one thing, namely the prohibition of (marrying) the daughter of the brother and the daughter of the sister, which he inferred by the analogy of the paternal and maternal aunts.

And also:

For example, [the Sadducees] prohibit divorce, although it is declared (by the Scripture) to be permissible. Also they make all months of thirty days; perhaps they rely in regard to this upon the story of Noah. They exclude the Sabbath from the number of the days of the feast of Passover, and observe the feast for seven days in addition to the Sabbath; likewise, in regard to the feast of Tabernacles . . . Daūd ibn Marwān al-Muqammiṣ treats . . . of some of their doctrines; we shall mention them at the end of the following chapter.[16]

[15] See S. Schechter, *op. cit.*, I, xviii–xxi; and recently, S. Zeitlin, *op. cit.*, 22–23.

[16] As quoted in L. Nemoy, "Al-Qirqisānī's Account of the Jewish Sects and Christianity," *HUCA*, Vol. VII (1930), 326 and 363.

Four statements in these quotations from Kirkisānī's work seem to refer to the Damascus Covenanters and the CDC. First, that Zadok opposed the Rabbanites and disagreed with them, could certainly be said of the Damascus Covenanters, who were the "sons of Zadok" (CDC, VI, 2), for they fiercely attacked the Pharisees of their time.[17] Secondly, the statement that Zadok did not support by props the laws he laid down except in forbidding a man to marry his niece, seems to refer to CDC, VII, 9–10. That the followers of Zadok prohibited divorce is corroborated by CDC, VII, 1 ff. And finally, the calendar of the Zadokites, as described by Kirkisānī, is identical with that of Jubilees, which, as we have pointed out, was the calendar of the Qumrān community and the Damascus Covenanters.

But of even greater interest in the light of the recent cave discoveries at Qumrān is Kirkisānī's reference to a certain cave sect, whom he calls the "Magharians," from the Arabic word for "cave." He describes them as follows:

Thereupon appeared the teaching of a sect called Magharians; they were called so because their (sacred) books were found in a cave. One of them is the Alexandrian whose book is famous and (widely) known; it is the most important of the books of the Magharians. Next to it (in importance) is a small booklet entitled "The Book of Yaddua," also a fine work. As for the rest of the Magharian books, most of them are of no value and resemble mere tales.[18]

Kirkisānī unfortunately does not give the ancient name of this sect; but, by describing them just after the Sadducees and before the Christians he places them chronologically in the period when the Qumrān sect flourished. Also the fact that he refers to their books having been found in a cave makes it very likely that this cave sect may have been the Qumrān community on the shore of the Dead Sea.

The same sect is mentioned by two Moslem authors, al-Bīrūnī

[17] Cf. S. Schechter, *op. cit.,* I, xvi–xviii.

[18] Nemoy, *op. cit.,* 326–327. Cf. also Kirkisānī's account of the doctrines of the Magharians (363–364). The Magharians may well be the same as the "followers of Zadok" (i.e., the Sadducees) mentioned above.

(973–1048) and Shahrastānī (1071–1153).[19] Shahrastānī's statement is especially interesting: "Arius, who affirmed that the Messiah is (the angel of God) and the elected of the created world,
took his theory from the members of this Sect [i.e., the cave sect],
who lived four hundred years before Arius and who devoted themselves to practising temperance and living a simple life." Again,
the chronology (Arius died A.D. 326) and the description of the life
of the sect seem to indicate that the writer is referring to the
Qumrān community.

The question naturally arises at this point why we should find
references to a cave sect, presumably the Qumrān sect, in the works
of Jewish and Moslem authors who lived a thousand years or more
after the sect disappeared from history. The answer may be found
in a Syriac letter from Timotheus I, Nestorian Patriarch of Seleucia
(726–819), to Sergius, the Metropolitan of Elam, about the discovery of some manuscripts in a cave near the Dead Sea about
A.D. 800. The letter is in part as follows:

We have learnt from trustworthy Jews who were then being instructed as catechumens in the Christian religion that some books
were found ten years ago in a rock-dwelling near Jericho. The story was
that the dog of an Arab out hunting, while in pursuit of game, went
into a cave and did not come out again; its owner went in after it and
found a chamber, in which there were many books, in the rock. The
hunter went off to Jerusalem and told his story to the Jews, who came
out in great numbers and found books of the Old Testament and
others in the Hebrew script; and, since there was a scholar well-read
in literature among them, I asked him about many passages which are
quoted in our New Testament (as) from the Old Testament but are
not found anywhere in it, neither (in copies found) amongst the Jews
nor (in those found) amongst Christians . . . but that Hebrew said
to me, "We have found more than 200 Psalms of David among our
books." [20]

[19] See R. de Vaux, "A propos des manuscrits de la Mer morte," *RB*, LVII
(1950), 417–429, for references.
[20] See O. Braun, "Ein Brief des Katholikos Timotheos I über biblische
Studien des 9 Jahrhunderts," in *Oriens Christianus*, I (1901), 299 ff. English
translation in G. R. Driver, *The Hebrew Scrolls* (London, 1951), 25–26.

There is a strong possibility that the cave which the Patriarch mentions may be Cave 1 of Qumrān, and that his letter may explain why so few manuscripts were found when it was discovered in 1947. At any rate, it is probable that behind the references to the cave sect by Kirkisānī and others is the discovery of the cave with the manuscripts, related by Timotheus.

This discovery may also solve the problem noted above of the relation of CDC to the teachings of the Karaites, who arose several centuries after CDC was written. For if a copy of CDC had been discovered with the other manuscripts at the time described by Timotheus—a fragment of CDC was discovered in Cave 6 of Qumrān, it will be remembered—it could well have been "recopied and circulated among the Karaites, whence copies might have been carried down into Egypt to be found there in the Genizah." [21]

[21] So H. H. Rowley, *The Zadokite Fragments and the Dead Sea Scrolls* (New York, 1952), 26. Cf. also P. Kahle, "The Age of the Scrolls," *VT*, I (1951), 38–48.

CHAPTER VII

The Qumrān Community and the Essenes

IT is hoped that this study of the excavations at Khirbet Qumrān and the manuscripts from the caves may have given the reader a clear picture of the history, life, and teachings of the Qumrān sect. It is now necessary to deal with the relation of this group with one of the most important sects in Judaism: the Essenes,[1] who flourished between the second century B.C. and the second century A.D.

An interesting passage in Pliny's *Natural History* describes a group of Essenes by the Dead Sea:

On the west side of the Dead Sea, but out of range of the noxious exhalations of the coast, is the solitary tribe of the Essenes, which is remarkable beyond all the other tribes in the whole world, as it has no women and has renounced all sexual desire, has no money, and has only palm-trees for company. Day by day the throng of refugees is recruited to an equal number by numerous accessions of persons tired of life and driven thither by the waves of fortune to adopt their manners. Thus

---

[1] The origin of the word "Essene," as well as of the sect itself, is still in dispute. K. Cook in *The Fathers of Jesus* (2 vols., London, 1886) II, 48–49, lists more than twenty-five different etymologies of the word. It may be connected with the Syriac word *hesē* ("holy, just, pure"): cf. Philo's explanation of its meaning as "holy, pious ones" (Greek, *hosioi*). The sect may be traced back to Mesopotamia, whence it migrated to Palestine after the Maccabean victories. This would account for the non-Jewish elements in its teachings. So, W. F. Albright, *From the Stone Age to Christianity* (Baltimore, 1940), 289.

through thousands of ages (incredible to relate) a race in which no one is born lives on for ever: so prolific for their advantage is other men's weariness of life!

Lying below the Essenes was formerly the town of Engedi, second only to Jerusalem in the fertility of its land and in its groves of palm-trees, but now like Jerusalem a heap of ashes. Next comes Masada, a fortress on a rock, itself also not far from the Dead Sea. This is the limit of Judaea.[2]

Dio Chrysostom, also of the first Christian century, is named by Synesius as praising the Essenes "for the happiness of their entire city which is situated near the Dead Sea, in the heart of Palestine, not far from Sodom." [3]

The question immediately arises whether Pliny and Dio were referring to the Qumrān community on the plateau to the west of the Dead Sea. The identification becomes almost certain if, as Dupont-Sommer has suggested,[4] Pliny's phrase "lying below the Essenes" is to be taken as meaning "south of the Essenes." In that case, Pliny would be stating that Engedi had been south of the Essenes, i.e., of Qumrān—which was true—and that Masada was next beyond Engedi. In this way Pliny mentioned the three important sites on the west shore of the Dead Sea in order from north to south: the city of the Essenes (Qumrān), Engedi, and Masada.

The main sources of information concerning the Essenes are Philo Judaeus and Josephus, both of whom wrote in the first century after Christ. It may be well to quote them in full for ready reference in the comparative study of the two sects which follows.

There are two extant statements by Philo. The first and longer occurs in the treatise "Quod Omnis Probus Liber Sit" (Every Good Man Is Free). To prove that the world is not altogether destitute of virtue, he cites an example from his own people:

---

[2] Pliny, *Natural History*, V, xv (as transl. by H. Rackham in the 10 vol. Loeb Classical Library ed., II, 277).

[3] Synesius, *Opera* (1864—in *Patrologia graeca*, ed. J. P. Migne, Vol. LXVI), 1119.

[4] A. Dupont-Sommer, *The Dead Sea Scrolls*, transl. by E. Margaret Rowley (Oxford and New York, 1952), 86 n.

XII. Palestinian Syria, too, has not failed to produce high moral excellence. In this country live a considerable part of the very populous nation of the Jews, including as it is said, certain persons, more than four thousand in number, called Essenes. Their name which is, I think, a variation, though the form of the Greek is inexact, of *hosiotēs* (holiness), is given them, because they have shown themselves especially devout in the service of God, not by offering sacrifices of animals, but by resolving to sanctify their minds. The first thing about these people is that they live in villages and avoid the cities because of the iniquities which have become inveterate among city dwellers, for they know that their company would have a deadly effect upon their own souls, like a disease brought by a pestilential atmosphere. Some of them labour on the land and others pursue such crafts as co-operate with peace and so benefit themselves and their neighbours. They do not hoard gold and silver or acquire great slices of land because they desire the revenues therefrom, but provide what is needed for the necessary requirements of life. For while they stand almost alone in the whole of mankind in that they have become moneyless and landless by deliberate action rather than by lack of good fortune, they are esteemed exceedingly rich, because they judge frugality with contentment to be, as indeed it is, an abundance of wealth. As for darts, javelins, daggers, or the helmet, breastplate or shield, you could not find a single manufacturer of them, nor, in general, any person making weapons or engines or plying any industry concerned with war, nor, indeed, any of the peaceful kind, which easily lapse into vice, for they have not the vaguest idea of commerce either wholesale or retail or marine, but pack the inducements to covetousness off in disgrace. Not a single slave is to be found among them, but all are free, exchanging services with each other, and they denounce the owners of slaves, not merely for their injustice in outraging the law of equality, but also for their impiety in annulling the statute of Nature, who mother-like has born and reared all men alike, and created them genuine brothers, not in mere name, but in very reality, though this kinship has been put to confusion by the triumph of malignant covetousness, which has wrought estrangement instead of affinity and enmity instead of friendship. As for philosophy they abandon the logical part to quibbling verbalists as unnecessary for the acquisition of virtue, and the physical to visionary praters as beyond the grasp of human nature, only retaining that part which treats philosophically of the existence of God and the creation of the universe. But the ethical part they study very industriously, taking for their trainers the laws of their fathers, which could not possibly have been conceived by the human soul without divine inspiration.

In these they are instructed at all other times, but particularly on the seventh days. For that day has been set apart to be kept holy and on it they abstain from all other work and proceed to sacred spots which they call synagogues. There, arranged in rows according to their ages, the younger below the elder, they sit decorously as befits the occasion with attentive ears. Then one takes the books and reads aloud and another of especial proficiency comes forward and expounds what is not understood. For most of their philosophical study takes the form of allegory, and in this they emulate the tradition of the past. They are trained in piety, holiness, justice, domestic and civic conduct, knowledge of what is truly good, or evil, or indifferent, and how to choose what they should and avoid the opposite, taking for their defining standards these three, love of God, love of virtue, love of men. Their love of God they show by a multitude of proofs, by religious purity constant and unbroken throughout their lives, by abstinence from oaths, by veracity, by their belief that the Godhead is the cause of all good things and nothing bad; their love of virtue, by their freedom from the love of either money or reputation or pleasure, by self-mastery and endurance, again by frugality, simple living, contentment, humility, respect for law, steadiness and all similar qualities; their love of men by benevolence and sense of equality, and their spirit of fellowship, which defies description, though a few words on it will not be out of place. First of all then no one's house is his own in the sense that it is not shared by all, for besides the fact that they dwell together in communities, the door is open to visitors from elsewhere who share their convictions.

Again they all have a single treasury and common disbursements; their clothes are held in common and also their food through their institution of public meals. In no other community can we find the custom of sharing roof, life and board more firmly established in actual practice. And that is no more than one would expect. For all the wages which they earn in the day's work they do not keep as their private property, but throw them into the common stock and allow the benefit thus accruing to be shared by those who wish to use it. The sick are not neglected because they cannot provide anything, but have the cost of their treatment lying ready in the common stock, so that they can meet expenses out of the greater wealth in full security. To the elder men too is given the respect and care which real children give to their parents, and they receive from countless hands and minds a full and generous maintenance for their latter years.

XIII. Such are the athletes of virtue produced by a philosophy free from the pedantry of Greek wordiness, a philosophy which sets its pupils to practise themselves in laudable actions, by which the liberty which can never be enslaved is firmly established. Here we have a proof. Many are the potentates who at various occasions have raised themselves to power over the country. They differed both in nature and the line of conduct which they followed. Some of them carried their zest for outdoing wild beasts in ferocity to the point of savagery. They left no form of cruelty untried. They slaughtered their subjects wholesale, or like cooks carved them piecemeal and limb by limb whilst still alive, and did not stay their hands till justice who surveys human affairs visited them with the same calamities. Others transformed this wild frenzy into another kind of viciousness. Their conduct showed intense bitterness, but they talked with calmness, though the mask of their milder language failed to conceal their rancorous disposition. They fawned like venomous hounds yet wrought evils irremediable and left behind them throughout the cities the unforgettable sufferings of their victims as monuments of their impiety and inhumanity. Yet none of these, neither the extremely ferocious nor the deep-dyed treacherous dissemblers, were able to lay a charge against this congregation of Essenes or holy ones here described. Unable to resist the high excellence of these people, they all treated them as self-governing and freemen by nature and extolled their communal meals and that ineffable sense of fellowship, which is the clearest evidence of a perfect and supremely happy life.[5]

Philo's longer work, "Apology for the Jews," of which only fragments are preserved in Eusebius' *Praeparatio Evangelica*, VIII, 11, contains the following description of the Essenes:

[5] Philo, as transl. by F. H. Colson in the 10-vol. *Loeb Classical Library* ed., IX, 53–63.

Our lawgiver trained into fellowship great numbers of pupils, who bear the name of Essenes (Essaioi), being, I imagine, honoured with the appellation by virtue of their holiness.

They dwell in many cities of Judæa and in many villages, and in large and populous communities.

Their order does not depend upon natural descent—for natural descent is not a right expression for what is voluntarily taken up—but proceeds from an earnest pursuit after virtue and yearning after love of mankind.

Among the Essenes there is, correctly speaking, no one altogether an infant, neither moreover youth with budding beard, nor boy; for the dispositions of such as these are unstable and subject to serious change owing to the immaturity of their age; but they consist of men matured and already verging upon old age, men flooded no longer by afflux of what is corporeal, nor led away by the passions, but in the very harvest time of the genuine and only absolute freedom.

The test of their freedom is their life. Not one of them can abide to be possessor of anything whatever as his own private property, whether house, or slave, or territory, or cattle, or any other of the things which constitute the apparatus or equipment of wealth. But once for all they lay all down in the midst, and reap their harvest from the common prosperity of all. They dwell, too, in the same fashion, in companies, making for themselves clubs and messes, and consistently do all business for the common weal. But the different members have different occupations, at which, like rivals, they engage with untiring energy, never making cold or heat, or any fluctuations of the weather, a pretence of excuse. They betake themselves to their customary works before the sun rises, and scarcely leave off when he sets, finding in them no less zest than those who show their strength in the gymnastic contests. For they deem the employments which they follow to be exercises more beneficial to life, and pleasanter to soul and to body, and more enduring, than any in the games, since they do not fall into desuetude with the bodily prime. Some among them are husbandmen, those who are well skilled in sowing and agriculture. Others again are herdsmen, managers of all kinds of cattle. Some of them are superintendents of hives of bees. Others are artificers in the crafts, for they neglect nothing in the way of innocent provision, so as never to be subjected to the hard compulsion of constraining needs. From these sources, so widely differing, they each get their wage, and hand it over to the steward regularly elected. He takes it and presently buys necessaries, and furnishes food without stint, and such other things as are absolute necessities of human subsistence. They live together and mess together every day, and find satisfaction in the same things, being lovers of contentment with little, and averse from extravagance as a disease of soul and body. Not only have they a common table, but also raiment in common. For they have ready in store for winter felted wool cloaks, and for summer easy vests without sleeves, and whoever wishes may conveniently take whichever he chooses; for what belongs to one is deemed to belong to all, and what belongs to all to each. Should any one of them, too, fall ill, he is medicined from the common store, and is tended with the attention and concern of all. And in fact their old men, even though they happen to be childless, are accustomed to close their lives in a most prosperous and comfortable old age, as if they not only were possessed of many children, but were blest with good ones; for they are looked upon as objects of provident regard and honour, by such as deem it their duty to care for them, and rather from voluntary inclination than from any tie of nature. Furthermore, seeing with more than ordinary quickness of perception what would be the only or the chief thing likely to break up the community, they deprecate marriage, and at the same time exercise an especial self-mastery.

Indeed no one of the Essenes marries a wife, because the wife is a selfish creature, immoderately smitten with jealousy, and terrible at shaking to their foundations the natural habits of a man, and bringing him under power by continual beguilements. For, as she practises fair false speeches, and other kinds of hypocrisy, as it were upon the stage, when she has succeeded in alluring eyes and ears, like cheated servants, she brings cajolery to bear upon the sovereign mind.

Moreover, if there are children, she begins to be puffed up with pride and licence of tongue; and all the things which before she speciously uttered in a disguised manner in irony, she now summons forth with a more daring confidence, and shamelessly forces her way into actions, every one of which is hostile to communion. For the man who is bound under spells of wife or children, being made anxious by the bond of nature, is no longer the same person towards others, but is entirely changed, having become, without being aware of it, a slave instead of a free man.

As above described, then, is their way of life—a life worth struggling after, and such that not only private persons but even great kings have been smitten with jealousy and wonder at these men, and add to their dignity still more by approbation and honours.[6]

Josephus refers to the Essenes many times throughout his works, but he describes their organization and teachings most fully in the following two passages:

2. For there are three philosophical sects among the Jews. The followers of the first of which are the Pharisees, of the second the Sadducees, and the third sect, which pretends to a severer discipline, are called Essens. These last are Jews by birth, and seem to have a greater affection for one another than the other sects have. These Essens reject pleasures as an evil, but esteem continence, and the conquest over our passions, to be virtue. They neglect wedlock, but choose out other persons' children, while they are pliable, and fit for learning, and esteem them to be of their kindred, and form them according to their own manners. They do not absolutely deny the fitness of marriage, and the succession of mankind thereby continued; but they guard against the lascivious behaviour of women, and are persuaded that none of them preserve their fidelity to one man.

3. These men are despisers of riches, and so very communicative as raises our admiration. Nor is there any one to be found among them who hath more than another; for it is a law among them, that those who come to them must let what they have be common to the whole order, insomuch that among them all there is no appearance of poverty or excess of riches, but every one's possessions are intermingled with every other's possessions, and so there is, as it were, one patrimony among all the brethren. They think that oil is a defilement; and if any one of them be anointed, without his own approbation, it is wiped off his body; for they think to be sweaty is a good thing, as they do also to be clothed in white garments. They also have stewards appointed to take care of their common affairs, who every one of them have no separate business for any, but what is for the uses of them all.

[6] As translated in K. Cook, *The Fathers of Jesus*, II, 5-8.

4. They have no one certain city, but many of them dwell in every city; and if any of their sect come from other places, what they have lies open for them, just as if it were their own, and they go into such as they never knew before, as if they had been ever so long acquainted with them. For which reason they carry nothing at all with them when they travel into remote parts, though still they take their weapons with them, for fear of thieves. Accordingly, there is, in every city where they live, one appointed particularly to take care of strangers, and to provide garments and other necessaries for them. But the habit and management of their bodies is such as children use who are in fear of their masters. Nor do they allow of the change of garments, or of shoes, till they be first entirely torn to pieces, or worn out by time. Nor do they either buy or sell any thing to one another, but every one of them gives what he hath to him that wanteth it, and receives from him again in lieu of it what may be convenient for himself; and although there be no requital made, they are fully allowed to take what they want of whomsoever they please.

5. And as for their piety towards God, it is very extraordinary; for before sun-rising they speak not a word about profane matters, but put up certain prayers, which they have received from their forefathers, as if they made a supplication for its rising. After this every one of them are sent away by their curators to exercise some of those arts wherein they are skilled, in which they labour with great diligence till the fifth hour. After which they assemble themselves together again into one place; and when they have clothed themselves in white veils, they then bathe their bodies in cold water. And after this purification is over, they every one meet together in an apartment of their own, into which it is not permitted to any of another sect to enter; while they go, after a pure manner, into the dining-room, as into a certain holy temple, and quietly set themselves down; upon which the baker lays them loaves in order; the cook also brings a single plate of one sort of food, and sets it before every one of them; but a priest says grace before meat; and it is unlawful for any one to taste of the food before grace be said. The same priest, when he hath dined, says grace again after meat, and when they begin, and when they end, they praise God, as he that bestows their food upon them; after which they lay aside their [white] garments, and betake themselves to their labours again till the evening; then they return home to supper, after the

same manner, and if there be any strangers there, they sit down with them. Nor is there ever any clamour or disturbance to pollute their house, but they give every one leave to speak in their turn; which silence thus kept in their house, appears to foreigners like some tremendous mystery; the cause of which is that perpetual sobriety they exercise, and the same settled measure of meat and drink that is allotted them, and that such as is abundantly sufficient for them.

6. And truly, as for other things, they do nothing but according to the injunctions of their curators; only these two things are done among them at every one's own free will, which are to assist those that want it, and to show mercy; for they are permitted of their own accord to afford succour to such as deserve it, when they stand in need of it, and to bestow food on those that are in distress; but they cannot give any thing to their kindred without the curators. They dispense their anger after a just manner, and restrain their passion. They are eminent for fidelity, and are the ministers of peace; whatsoever they say also is firmer than an oath; but swearing is avoided by them, and they esteem it worse than perjury; for they say, that he who cannot be believed without [swearing by] God, is already condemned. They also take great pains in studying the writings of the ancients, and choose out of them what is most for the advantage of their soul and body, and they inquire after such roots and medicinal stones as may cure their distempers.

7. But now, if any one hath a mind to come over to their sect, he is not immediately admitted, but he is prescribed the same method of living which they use, for a year, while he continues excluded, and they give him a small hatchet, and the forementioned girdle, and the white garment. And when he hath given evidence, during that time, that he can observe their continence, he approaches nearer to their way of living, and is made a partaker of the waters of purification; yet is he not even now admitted to live with them; for after this demonstration of his fortitude, his temper is tried two more years, and if he appear to be worthy, they then admit him into their society. And before he is allowed to touch their common food, he is obliged to take tremendous oaths, that, in the first place, he will exercise piety towards God, and then that he will observe justice towards men, and that he will do no harm to any one, either of his own accord, or by the command of

others; that he will always hate the wicked, and be assistant to the righteous; that he will ever show fidelity to all men, and especially to those in authority, because no one obtains the government without God's assistance; and that if he be in authority, he will at no time whatever abuse his authority, nor endeavour to outshine his subjects, either in his garments, or any other finery; that he will be perpetually a lover of truth, and propose to himself to reprove those that tell lies; that he will keep his hands clear from theft, and his soul from unlawful gains; and that he will neither conceal any thing from those of his own sect, nor discover any of their doctrines to others, no, not though any one should compel him so to do at the hazard of his life. Moreover, he swears to communicate their doctrines to no one any otherwise than as he received them himself; that he will abstain from robbery, and will equally preserve the books belonging to their sect, and the names of the angels [or messengers]. These are the oaths by which they secure their proselytes to themselves.

8. But for those that are caught in any heinous sins, they cast them out of their society, and he who is thus separated from them, does often die after a miserable manner; for as is bound by the oath he hath taken, and by the customs he hath been engaged in, he is not at liberty to partake of that food that he meets with elsewhere, but is forced to eat grass, and to famish his body with hunger till he perish; for which reason they receive many of them again, when they are at their last gasp, out of compassion to them, as thinking the miseries they have endured till they came to the very brink of death, to be a sufficient punishment for the sins they had been guilty of.

9. But in the judgments they exercise they are most accurate and just, nor do they pass sentence by the votes of a court that is fewer than a hundred. And as to what is once determined by that number it is unalterable. What they most of all honour, after God himself, is the name of their legislator [Moses], whom if any one blaspheme, he is punished capitally. They also think it a good thing to obey thier elders, and the major part. Accordingly, if ten of them be sitting together, no one of them will speak while the other nine are against it. They also avoid spitting in the midst of them, or on the right side. Moreover, they are stricter than any other of the Jews in resting from their labours on the seventh day; for they not only get their food ready the day before, that they may not be obliged to kindle a fire on that day, but

they will not remove any vessel out of its place, nor go to stool thereon. Nay, on other days they dig a small pit, a foot deep, with a paddle (which kind of hatchet is given them, when they are first admitted among them), and covering themselves round with their garment, that they may not affront the divine rays of light, they ease themselves into that pit, after which they put the earth that was dug out again into the pit; and even this they do only in the more lonely places, which they choose out for this purpose; and although this easement of the body be natural, yet it is a rule with them to wash themselves after it, as if it were a defilement to them.

10. Now after the time of their preparatory trial is over, they are parted into four classes; and so far are the juniors inferior to the seniors, that if the seniors should be touched by the juniors, they must wash themselves, as if they had intermixed themselves with the company of a foreigner. They are long-lived also, insomuch that many of them live above a hundred years, by means of the simplicity of their diet, nay, as I think, by means of the regular course of life they observe also. They contemn the miseries of life, and are above pain, by the generosity of their mind. And as for death, if it will be for their glory, they esteem it better than living always; and indeed our war with the Romans gave abundant evidence what great souls they had in their trials, wherein, although they were tortured and distorted, burnt and torn to pieces, and went through all kinds of instruments of torment, that they might be forced either to blaspheme their legislator, or to eat what was forbidden them, yet they could not be made to do either of them, no, nor once to flatter their tormentors, or to shed a tear; but they smiled in their very pains, and laughed those to scorn who inflicted the torments upon them, and resigned up their souls with great alacrity, as expecting to receive them again.

11. For their doctrine is this, That bodies are corruptible, and that the matter they are made of is not permanent; but that the souls are immortal, and continue for ever, and that they come out of the most subtile air; and are united to their bodies as to prisons, into which they are drawn by a certain natural enticement; but that when they are set free from the bonds of the flesh, they then, as released from a long bondage, rejoice and mount upward. And this is like the opinion of the Greeks, that good souls have their habitations beyond the ocean, in a region that is neither oppressed with storms of rain, or snow, or with

intense heat, but that this place is such as is refreshed by the gentle breathing of a west wind, that is perpetually blowing from the ocean; while they allot to bad souls a dark and tempestuous den, full of never-ceasing punishments. And indeed the Greeks seem to me to have followed the same notion, when they allot the islands of the blessed to their brave men, whom they call heroes and demigods; and to the souls of the wicked, the region of the ungodly, in Hades, where their fables relate that certain persons, such as Sisyphus and Tantalus, and Ixion and Tityus, are punished; which is built on this first supposition, that souls are immortal, and thence are those exhortations to virtue, and dehortations from wickedness collected, whereby good men are bettered in the conduct of their life by the hope they have of reward after their death, and whereby the vehement inclinations of bad men to vice are restrained, by the fear and expectation they are in, that although they should lie concealed in this life, they should suffer immortal punishment after their death. These are the divine doctrines of the Essens about the soul, which lay an unavoidable bait for such as have once had a taste of their philosophy.

12. There are also those among them who undertake to foretell things to come, by reading the holy books, and using several sorts of purifications, and being perpetually conversant in the discourses of the prophets; and it is but seldom that they miss in their predictions.

13. Moreover, there is another order of Essens, who agree with the rest as to their way of living, and customs, and laws, but differ from them in the point of marriage, as thinking that by not marrying they cut off the principal part of human life, which is the prospect of succession; nay rather, that if all men should be of the same opinion, the whole race of mankind would fail. However, they try their spouses for three years; and if they find that they have their natural purgations thrice, as trials that they are likely to be fruitful, they then actually marry them. But they do not use to accompany with their wives when they are with child, as a demonstration that they do not marry out of regard to pleasure, but for the sake of posterity. Now the women go into the baths with some of their garments on, as the men do with somewhat girded about them. And these are the customs of this order of Essens.[7]

[7] WJ, II, viii.

And again:

5. The doctrine of the Essens is this, That all things are best ascribed to God. They teach the immortality of souls, and esteem that the rewards of righteousness are to be earnestly striven for; and when they send what they have dedicated to God into the temple, they do not offer sacrifices, because they have more pure lustrations of their own; on which account they are excluded from the common court of the temple, but offer their sacrifices themselves; yet is their course of life better than that of other men; and they entirely addict themselves to husbandry. It also deserves our admiration, how much they exceed all other men that addict themselves to virtue, and this in righteousness; and indeed to such a degree, that as it hath never appeared among any other men, neither Greeks nor barbarians, no, not for a little time, so hath it endured a long while among them. This is demonstrated by that institution of theirs which will not suffer any thing to hinder them from having all things in common; so that a rich man enjoys no more of his own wealth than he who hath nothing at all. There are about four thousand men that live in this way, and neither marry wives, nor are desirous to keep servants; as thinking the latter tempts men to be unjust, and the former gives the handle to domestic quarrels; but as they live by themselves, they minister one to another. They also appoint certain stewards to receive the incomes of their revenues, and of the fruits of the ground; such as are good men and priests, who are to get their corn and their food ready for them. They none of them differ from others of the Essens in their way of living, but do the most resemble those Dacæ who are called Polistai [dwellers in cities].[8]

After reading Philo's and Josephus' accounts of the Essenes,[9] one is struck by the many similarities between their practices and teachings and those of the Qumrān sect. It is our purpose now to discuss some of the more important of these similarities, as well as some of the differences, between these two groups.

[8] AJ, XVIII, i, 5.

[9] Josephus says that when he was sixteen he decided to try out the three important sects of Judaism, the Pharisees, Sadducees, and Essenes. "For I thought that by this means I might choose the best, if I were once acquainted with them all; so I contented myself with hard fare, and underwent great difficulties and went through them all." *Life of Josephus*, 2.

Both Philo and Josephus mention that in their day about four thousand Essenes lived in the cities and villages of Judea, and that regularly elected officials, called "stewards" or "curators," were in charge of their affairs. According to CDC, XV, 4, the Damascus Covenanters were divided into thousands, hundreds, fifties, and tens (cf. also 1QS, II, 21–22), and over each such "camp" there was a *mebaqqer*, or Supervisor (CDC, XVI, 1). A *mebaqqer* also was at the head of the Qumrān community (1QS, VI, 12). The Essenes have been thought to be a monastic sect, practicing the strictest celibacy—as Pliny reported in the first century. Josephus, however, described a group among them who practiced a kind of marriage by trial, merely for the propagation of their own kind. The Qumrān sect may have belonged to this group, because women and children are mentioned in the unpublished fragment of 1QS [10] and skeletons of women have been found in the cemetery beside the Khirbeh. CDC, VII, seems to indicate that marriage was permissible for the members of the sect.

Josephus' description of the various stages of initiation into the Essene order is strikingly similar to the description in 1QS, V, 1, to VI, 23. After one year of probation—the exact length of the period is not designated in 1QS—the Essene novitiate was admitted into the waters of purification. Then came two years of testing, after which he took a fearful oath and was admitted to the communal meal. During this period of initiation, he received a small hatchet, a loincloth for bathing, and a white garment, a part of the ceremony not mentioned in 1QS.

Another mark of similarity is the communal life practiced by the two groups. The communal meal, the community of goods, and the democratic character are essential both to the Essenes and the Qumrān community.

Philo very carefully stresses the equality that prevailed among the Essenes, pointing out that not a single slave was to be found among them. This also prevailed in the Qumrān sect, each mem-

[10] See pp. 31–32.

ber of which was allowed to express his opinion and vote in the session of the many (1QS, VI, 19).

Josephus' description of the Essenes' communal meal is more detailed than that found in 1QS, VI, 4–6; but the Manual adds the important detail of the blessing of the bread and wine by the priest, which denotes the sacramental character of the meal. The Essenes also bathed their bodies in cold water before each meal, according to Josephus. It was no doubt such lustral rites that made necessary so many reservoirs of all sizes at the Qumrān community center.

The orderliness, quietness, and decorum of the Essene assemblies made a strong impression on both Philo and Josephus. They are even more clearly brought out by the description in the Qumrān Manual (VI, 8–13) of the session of the many.

A curious similarity between the Essenes and the Qumrān community is in the rule concerning spitting. Josephus writes that the Essenes "avoid spitting in the midst of them, or on the right side," and the Manual states that "anyone who spits into the midst of the session of the many shall be fined for thirty days" (VII, 13). It is remarkable that this small point recorded by Josephus should be corroborated in the Qumrān Manual.

He also reports that banishment from the Essene community of members caught in any heinous sins often led to a miserable death from starvation, since the vigorous vows they had taken forbade them to eat ordinary food. 1QS also mentions eternal banishment from the community for open or secret transgressors of the Torah, without describing the sinner's end (VIII, 20, to IX, 2).

Not only many practices of the Essenes but also many of their teachings agree with those of the Qumrān sect, as the following study will show.

The teachings not only of the Essenes, as described by Philo and Josephus, but of the Qumrān sect stress such basic ideas as righteousness, holiness, purity, truth and piety. Knowledge and wisdom also are important in the theology of the two groups.

The special interest of the Essenes in the Bible and in the books of the ancients is significant in the light of the huge library of manuscripts discovered at Qumrān. Philo writes that the Essenes were interested mainly in the ethical part of philosophy. They were trained in the laws of their fathers, which they believed were divinely inspired. In these they were instructed at all times, but especially on the seventh days. They sat in rows, according to their ages, listening attentively to the reading of the books and to the exposition of that which was not understood.

Josephus also tells us that the Essenes pored over the writings of the ancients, and chose out of them what was most advantageous for soul and body. New numbers of the sect had to swear, as part of the strict initiatory oath, that they would preserve the books which belonged to it. And he reports that there were those who foretold events by reading the holy books and being conversant with the Prophets.[11]

Like the Essenes, the members of the Qumrān community must have cherished their books and carefully preserved them. At any minute of the day or night some member or other would be reading or expounding the Torah. They were skilled in interpreting the utterances of the Prophets, as the Habakkuk Commentary shows. Philo remarks that the Essenes used allegorical principles of interpretation when dealing with the Scriptures; but we find little of this in the sectarian works from Qumrān.[12]

The theory of Essenic origin of such extracanonical books as Jubilees, Enoch, the Testaments of the Twelve Patriarchs, and the Assumption of Moses, held by certain scholars long before the Qumrān discoveries,[13] takes on new significance in the light of the close connection between the Essenes and the Qumrān community. There is strong reason to believe now that these works were produced by the Jewish sect that settled along the Dead Sea. Fragments of most of them have been found in the caves at Qumrān; previously unexplained passages in them have become clear through

[11] Cf. Herod's encounter with an Essene prophet in his youth, p. 24, n. 15.
[12] Cf. W. H. Brownlee, "Biblical Interpretation Among the Sectaries of the Dead Sea Scrolls," BA, XIV (1951), 54–76.
[13] Cf. A. Dupont-Sommer, The Dead Sea Scrolls, 94–95.

the study of the sectarian documents from Qumrān, and vice versa; and allusions to these works are found in the sectarian documents.[14] Since it has been shown quite conclusively from the many parallels cited in this chapter that the Qumrān sect were Essenes, or at least Essenic in character, it follows then that Jubilees, Enoch, the Testaments of the Twelve Patriarchs, and others, originated in Essenic literary circles.

However the problem of the relation between the Essenes and the Qumrān sect cannot be treated without noting some differences between the groups.

In the first place Philo and Josephus tell us a number of things about the Essenes which are not in the sectarian documents from Qumrān. This, of course, may be due simply to the fact that all of the material from Qumrān has not yet been published. To the more important points we give our attention now.

Josephus states that the Essene novitiate received a small hatchet (to bury his excrement), a loincloth (to use when bathing), and a white garment as wearing apparel. 1QS, VI, 13–23, describing the rules of admission into the community, mentions none of these.

The Essenes' interest in the study of roots and medicinal stones for the cure of distemper, and their secret knowledge of the names of angels, are not mentioned in the records from Qumrān.

Josephus describes the peculiar Essene custom of rising before dawn and facing the east to offer prayers as though for the rising of the sun. Whether this was the vestige of a kind of sun worship inherited from foreign sources, or merely an invocation prayer at the beginning of the day, we cannot definitely say. Nothing corresponds exactly with this practice in the sectarian documents from Qumrān, although morning and evening prayers are mentioned in 1QS, X, 10.

According to Philo, the Essenes were industrious. Some were skilled in agriculture, others in cattle raising; some were in charge of bees, others were craftsmen. For their work they received wages which they handed over to the steward of the group, and he bought

[14] CDC, *passim*, especially XX, 1.

the necessities for human subsistence. There is nothing of all this in the Qumrān texts, although CDC, XVIII, 1, mentions that the wages of two days in every month were given to the Supervisor for the needs of the community. We can be sure that the members of the Qumrān sect also worked in similar ways for their mutual support and for the welfare of the community.

In the second place, the differences between the two groups may seem more serious than they really are. Of the offering of sacrifices, for instance, Philo writes that the Essenes were especially devout in that they did not offer sacrifices of animals, but rather resolved to sanctify their minds. If this does not suggest condemnation of sacrifices, it at least implies a deeply spiritual attitude toward the whole sacrificial system which could easily cause complete abandonment of it. In CDC, however, the sect still considered the Temple in Jerusalem to be their Sanctuary, and took part in the sacrifices (XIII, 27), but only according to their own regulations (VIII, 12–20). To this Josephus notes that the Essenes did not offer sacrifices, because they had purer lustrations of their own; being excluded on that account from the common court of the Temple, they offered their sacrifices themselves outside. On this point there seems to be no disagreement between CDC and Josephus. 1QS, however, contains no regulations for the offering of sacrifices. The Qumrān community evidently believed that sacrifices were useless, and that a pure life was the best gift to God. This is expressed in a beautiful passage (1QS, IX, 3–5) steeped in the Old Testament Prophets:

When these things come to pass in Israel according to all these rules for the institution of the Holy Spirit according to eternal truth for making atonement for the guilt of transgression and sinful infidelity, and for (divine) favor for the land without [15] flesh of whole burnt offerings or the fat of sacrifices. But the offering of the lips according to justice is like the fragrance of righteousness and the perfection of way is like the free-will gift of an acceptable offering.

[15] Dupont-Sommer's rendering.

It may be that the Essenes who went into the desert to build their religious community at Qumrān broke completely with the Temple cult at Jerusalem and therefore did not offer animal sacrifices, whereas other Essene groups in the villages and cities of Palestine maintained a tenuous relationship with the Temple in Jerusalem such as CDC and Josephus describe. Or, CDC, and 1QS with its strong spiritualization of the sacrificial system, may represent two different stages in the history of the Qumrān sect —i.e., of the Essenes—of which Josephus describes one and Philo the other.

Philo's strong statement that the Essenes had nothing to do with arms, or the making of them, does not seem to fit in with the militant sect of 1QM, the document which describes the war between the children of light and the children of darkness. This scroll, found among the manuscripts of Qumrān, obviously refers to the battles waged by the Qumrān sect against its enemies. As we have noted, this warfare, even if we interpret it in an eschatological sense, was based on actual military practices by the sect against earthly enemies. This military handbook then may belong to an earlier period of the sect, perhaps the time of the Maccabean struggles, when enemies sought to subjugate it, whereas the more pacifistic Essenes described by Philo may have lived at a later time when military procedures were abandoned and submission was shown to those in authority.[16]

Another objection to identifying the Qumrān sect with the Essenes may be found in the fact that neither Philo nor Josephus touched on the Teacher of Righteousness and the Community of the New Covenant which he had founded. But it must be remembered that the Teacher of Righteousness was not the founder of the Essenes, but of a schismatic group within the Essenes. Dupont-

---

[16] Cf. Josephus' description of the great oaths of the Essene novitiate, in which he swore that he would show fidelity to those in authority, because it was only by God's assistance that they had received the right to govern. Members who were still militaristically inclined no doubt left the Essene party and joined the Zealots, who led the open revolt against the Romans in the first century after Christ.

Sommer suggests also that Josephus, who admired the Essenes so greatly, purposely avoided mentioning this great character because he had been condemned and executed by the Jews.[17] Whatever the reason for this omission, it is not serious enough to forbid identifying the Covenanters with the Essenes.

From this study of the organization and teachings of the Essenes and the Qumrān sect, it is clear that the similarities between them far outweigh the differences, and that any differences can be attributed either to prejudiced and faulty reporting by Philo and Josephus or to our own inadequate knowledge of the history and teachings of the Qumrān sect. Therefore we conclude that the Jewish, semimonastic, Covenant community of Qumrān is to be included under the term "Essene" in its widest sense as used by Josephus.

[17] A. Dupont-Sommer, *op. cit.*, 90–91. Cf. also Josephus' failure to mention the departure of the Qumrān sect from Palestine during the reign of Herod the Great, perhaps for a similar reason.

CHAPTER VIII

The Qumrān Community
and the New Testament

THE Qumrān manuscripts have already proved to be exceedingly valuable for Old Testament studies. The light they throw upon the Hebrew text and its history, the Greek translation of the Old Testament, the problem of canonization, Hebrew palaeography, and other disciplines related to the Old Testament field is truly remarkable.

Intertestamental studies have also benefited greatly. The revival of interest in this oft neglected field since the Qumrān discoveries augurs well for a better understanding and fuller knowledge of the theological and historical developments in Judaism between 200 B.C. and A.D. 200. Not only many of the Apocryphal and Pseudepigraphical works but many fragments of unknown works are represented among the manuscript fragments discovered at Qumrān. This material is already throwing new light not only on the perplexing problem of the original language of these intertestamental works, but also on many passages which heretofore have not been fully understood.

But it is in the field of New Testament studies that the Qumrān documents will prove to be especially significant. Some work has already been done and much more will be forthcoming as New Testament scholars increasingly realize the importance of the new finds.

Soon after the manuscripts of CDC were published G. Margoliouth suggested in 1910 that they might have originated from a

Judaeo-Christian sect in the first century.[1] This view, after a period
of eclipse, was taken up again in 1951 by Dr. J. L. Teicher of Cambridge in a series of articles in the *Journal of Jewish Studies*, suggesting that the Covenanters were an Ebionite Christian sect.[2] He
identified the Teacher of Righteousness with Jesus, and the Prophet
of Untruth with Paul. Another view, that would put our texts in
the same general period, identifies the Teacher of Righteousness
with John the Baptist, and gives the writings an anti-Christian
character.[3] But all theories which identify the Qumrān sect with
first-century movements are made untenable by the archaeological
and palaeographical evidence from Qumrān.

Let us now look at some of the more important phases of the
New Testament affected by the Qumrān discoveries.

John the Baptist

There is little doubt that John the Baptist was a key figure
through whom many of the practices and teachings of the Qumrān
sect found their way into early Christianity. As a lad, he left home
and dwelt in the desert of Judea "until the day of his showing unto
Israel" (Lk. 1:80). It has been suggested that he passed this period
with the Essenes, for Josephus tells us that "they neglect wedlock,
but choose out other persons' children, while they are pliable, and
fit for learning, and esteem them to be of their kindred, and form
them according to their own manners" (WJ, II, viii, 2).[4] It may
well be, in view of John's acquaintance with Essene thought, that
he lived with the ascetics during his early years and learned of
their manners and doctrines.

It was in this same wilderness of Judea, of course, that the

---

[1] Cf. "The Sadducean Christians of Damaskus," *Athenaeum*, Nov. 26, 1910,
657–659.
[2] Teicher, "The Dead Sea Scrolls—Documents of the Jewish-Christian Sect
of Ebionites" and "The Damascus Fragments and the Origin of the Jewish-
Christian Sect," JJS, II (1951), 67–99, 115–143.
[3] R. Eisler, "Hebrew Scrolls: Further Evidence for Their Pre-Christian
Date," *Modern Churchman*, XXXIX (1949), 284–287.
[4] Cf. the recent excellent article by Prof. Brownlee, "John the Baptist in the
New Light of Ancient Scrolls," *Interpretation*, IX (1955), 71–90.

Qumrān community had settled in accordance with its interpretation of Is. 40:3. "Now when these things come to pass in Israel to the Community, according to these rules, they will separate themselves from the midst of the session of perverse men to go to the wilderness to prepare there the way of HUHA [a surrogate for Yahweh], as it is written: 'In the wilderness clear the way . . . [name of Yahweh omitted here], Make level in the desert a highway for our God' " (1QS, VIII, 12–14).

Here they took up their communal way of life, separated from the world, believing that through the study of Torah and the practice of holy living they were preparing the way for the Messiah.

John became convinced that the Essenes were not fulfilling Is. 40:3, because they were preparing only themselves and not the nation as a whole for the coming of the Messiah; and so he left them and carried on a vigorous program of baptizing and preaching in the Jordan valley (John 1:28 and 3:23), in the belief that this did fulfill the prophecy of Isaiah and prepare the way for the Messiah.

The preaching message of John centered around the great theme of repentance. "Repent ye, for the kingdom of heaven is at hand" (Matt. 3:2—cf. also Mk. 1:4 and Lk. 3:3), were the startling words he spoke to those who came to hear him. Repentance was of course important in the Qumrān theology, for the members of the Qumrān sect believed that they belonged to a "covenant of repentance" (CDC, IX, 15[B]), and called themselves "those who repent of transgression" (CDC, II, 3, and IX, 41, and 1QS, X, 20), and "the penitents of Israel" (CDC, VI, 1, VIII, 6, IX, 24).

Baptism, John taught, was the outward sign of an inward change of heart, and he insisted that it be administered as such, to both proselytes and persons who were born Jews. "But when he saw many of the Pharisees and Sadducees come to his baptism, he said unto them, O generation of vipers, who hath warned you to flee from the wrath to come? Bring forth therefore fruits meet for repentance; and think not to say within yourselves, We have Abraham to our father: for I say unto you, that God is able of these stones to raise up children unto Abraham" (Matt. 3:7-9—cf. also Lk. 3:7-8). In other words, being a Jew—a child of Abraham—was not enough for entering the Kingdom. Only one who truly repented and was baptized could inherit the Kingdom.

This extreme indictment of the Jewish nation is characteristic also of the Qumrān sect, who regarded all men outside their group as belonging to the realm of Belial. They had separated themselves from the children of darkness by living in accordance with the Torah of Moses and by observing lustral rites. They were the true Israel, whose sins were atoned for through submission to God's holy ordinances, so that they, and they alone, could be sanctified by purifying water (1QS, III, 8-9). In other words, only for them could the baptismal rite have any meaning.

John's message also had a clear, Messianic note. He believed that he was preparing the way for the Messiah, even as the Covenanters did. The age of the Kingdom was nigh, and he was inviting the people to enter that Kingdom through repentance and baptism before the final day of judgment.

John, with all his Messianic fervor, never identified himself with the Messiah (John 1:20), for he considered himself to be only a "voice," that is, the herald of the Messiah. He pointed to the One who was mightier than he (Matt. 3:11), to the Lamb of God who takes away the sin of the world (John 1:29), and to the One whose shoe latchets he was unworthy to unloose (John 1:27). John baptized with water, but "he that cometh after me . . . shall baptize you with the Holy Ghost, and with fire: Whose fan is in his hand, and he will thoroughly purge his floor, and gather his wheat into the garner; but he will burn up the chaff with unquenchable fire" (Matt. 3:11–12). Baptism with fire, as explained in verse 12, obviously refers to the judgment which will come upon those who do not repent.

This judgment by fire is more fully described in one of the Qumrān hymns:

While the rope (of destruction) descended on the damned,
and the Destiny of anger on the abandoned,

and the overflowing of wrath on the outcasts,
and it was the time of Fury for all Belial.
And the bonds of Death surrounded so that there was no escape,
and the torrents of Belial overflowed all their banks.
The fire consumes all beings who draw from it,
causing to disappear from their rivers every tree, both green and
    withered;
and it lashes with whirlwinds of flame
until there is no longer any creature who drinks there.
It consumes the foundations of asphalt
and the base of the earth;
the foundations of the mountains are the prey of burning,
and the roots of flint become torrents of pitch.
And it consumes even as far as the Great Abyss,
and the torrents of Belial break into Abaddon,
and the creatures of the Abyss endowed with reason make their din
    resound
amongst the tumult of the eddies of mud.[5]

It may be that John had this description of the eschatological river
of fire in mind when he talked of the baptism of fire.

But what of the baptism of the Holy Ghost? This would seem
to refer to those who accepted John's message of repentance and
baptism, whereas the baptism by fire was reserved for those who did
not accept his message. This beneficial character of the baptism
of the Holy Spirit is clearly brought out in the Qumrān literature.
Not only does God "sprinkle upon him [the Messiah] the spirit of
truth as purifying water so as to cleanse him from all abominations
of falsehood and from being contaminated with the spirit of impurity" (1QS, IV, 21–22), but the Messiah himself sprinkles his
followers with his Holy Spirit and thus makes them his anointed
ones.[6] John the Baptist, according to the Fourth Gospel, clearly

---

[5] As translated in A. Dupont-Sommer, op. cit., 73.
[6] This seems to be the meaning of 1QS, IX, 11, which speaks of "the
anointed ones of Aaron and Israel," and of CDC, II, 9, which states that
"through his Messiah He shall make them know his Holy Spirit." In this
connection, Is. 52:15 must now be read, "So shall he sprinkle many nations,"
with AV.

expresses this dynamic aspect of the Messiah's work: "And I knew him not: but he that sent me to baptize with water, the same said unto me, Upon whom thou shalt see the Spirit descending, and remaining on him, the same is he which baptizeth with the Holy Ghost" (John 1:33).

John differed, however, from the Essenes, with whom he had such close ties, in two important ways. In the first place, he was a popular preacher, directing his message of repentance to the common man. This was certainly not the method used by the Essenes in recruiting members. Evidently their way of life was so challenging and satisfying in contrast with the corrupt religious and political conditions of the day that people were attracted to them without much urging. At any rate, we hear of no active program of evangelization by the Essenes to gain members.[7] John, on the other hand, felt impelled to go to the people with his message and proclaim aloud the coming of the Messiah.

In the second place, it became John's high privilege to prepare the way for the true Messiah. When Jesus came to him, John recognized him and cried, "Behold the Lamb of God, which taketh away the sin of the world" (John 1:29), and he baptized him. The Qumrān community, on the other hand, in spite of careful preparation and Messianic fervor, never recognized the true Messiah, as far as we know. The road which they had prepared in the desert was a dead end, for it never led for them to the Messiah. And yet their sincere devotion and passionate loyalty to the ordinances of God were not in vain. For one, who may have been a member of an Essenic group in his early life, and who was thoroughly acquainted with their teachings and Messianic hopes, was honored by God to prepare the way for his Anointed.

The Gospel of John

As Professor Brownlee remarks in his definitive study of John the Baptist and his relation to the Essenes, "the most astonishing

[7] However, as we have noted, Josephus wrote that they adopted children to train them in the ways of the sect.

result of all is the validation of the Fourth Gospel as an authentic source concerning the Baptist." [8] But, more than this, the language and ideas of the Fourth Gospel are so closely connected with Essene thought as represented in the Qumrān documents, that "one may *almost* say that in John's portrayal of Jesus we have the Essene Christ." [9] How do we account for these close links between John the Baptist and the writer of the Fourth Gospel, and between the Fourth Gospel and the Essene documents from Qumrān?

From certain passages in the Book of Acts we know that there were certain disciples in Ephesus who knew only of the baptism of John (Acts 18:24-26, 19:1-7), and that Paul and others, after telling them of the Messiah who came after John, baptized them in the name of the Lord Jesus. There is also a strong tradition that the Gospel of John was written at Ephesus, which could explain how the Evangelist came to know so much about John the Baptist and the Essene-Covenanter background out of which he came.

The parallels of language and thought between the Johannine writings and the sectarian documents from Qumrān, especially 1QS, are indeed striking. Rare phrases, like "works of God" (1QS, IV, 4) and "light of life" (1QS, III, 15), are used by Jesus in conversations recorded by John (John 6:8, 9:3, 8:12). Of the Logos, John writes, "All things were made by him; and without him was not anything made that was made" (1:3), which is closely paralleled by 1QS, XI, 11: "And by His knowledge everything has come into being, and everything that is by His purpose He established, and without Him nothing is done."

Far more significant are the numerous references in the Gospel of John to darkness and light, untruth and truth, which reflect a basic dualism very similar to that in the Dead Sea scrolls.[10] In John we find such expressions as "children of light" (12:36—cf. 1QS, I, 9–10), "spirit of truth" and "spirit of error" (I John 4:6—cf. 1QS, III, 18, and the designation of the Paraclete as the "spirit of truth"

[8] Brownlee, *op. cit.*, 89.
[9] *Ibid.*, 84.
[10] See pp. 70–73 for a discussion of the dualism in the Qumrān texts.

in John 14:17, 15:26, 16:13), "walking in the light" and "walking in darkness" (I John 1:6–7, 2:11, and John 8:12, 11:10, 12:35—cf. 1QS, III, 20–21). As our discussion of the dualism of the Qumrān documents has noted, the dualistic view of the world, especially in 1QS, had its origin in Iranian thought, which conceived of good and evil as coexistent forces in conflict for control of the world. In Judaism, however, God creates them and has control of them until the ultimate overthrow of evil. Professor Kuhn points out that John borrowed this dualism, which was ethical in character, as part of his world view. Therefore, "in these new texts we get hold of the fundamental source of John's Gospel, and this source is Palestinian-Jewish; not, however, Pharisaic-Rabbinic Judaism, but a Palestinian-Jewish pietistic Sect of gnostic structure." [11]

Jesus

The many striking resemblances between the Essenes and the early Christians [12] have led scholars to believe that there was an organic connection between Essenism and Christianity. It was also suggested that Jesus must have been an Essene, because He constantly inveighed against the Pharisees and Sadducees, but never against the Essenes, who formed the third great Jewish sect of His time.[13] But Bishop Lightfoot dealt a deathblow to these extreme views on the relation between Essenism and Christianity in his masterful dissertation "The Essenes." [14]

The discovery of the Qumrān documents, however, reopened the whole problem. Professor Dupont-Sommer, in his early work on the scrolls, was perhaps too enthusiastic when he wrote, "The Galilean Master, as He is presented to us in the writings of the New Testament, appears in many respects as an astonishing reincarnation of the Master of Justice," [15] listing a dozen or more simi-

[11] K. G. Kuhn, "Die in Palästina gefundenen hebräischen Texte und das Neue Testament," ZKT, XLVII (1950), 210.
[12] Cf. F. C. Conybeare, "Essenes," HDB, I, 770b.
[13] Cf. C. D. Ginsburg, The Essenes (London, 1864), 24.
[14] J. B. Lightfoot, Saint Paul's Epistles to the Colossians and to Philemon (6th ed., London, 1882), 349–419.
[15] A. Dupont-Sommer, The Dead Sea Scrolls (Oxford, 1952), 99.

larities between Jesus and the Teacher of Righteousness, and between the Christian Church and the "Essene Church." His initial ardor abated considerably with the appearance of his second work on the scrolls; [16] but he still holds, rightly, that the Jewish sect of the Covenant "directly and immediately prepared the way for the Christian Church, and that it helped to shape both the Church's soul and its body."

Let us look now at some of the similarities in teachings and organization between the Qumrān sect and Jesus and His Church.

Matthew tells us (7:28–29) of the Sermon on the Mount that "the people were astonished at his doctrine, for he taught them as one having authority, and not as the scribes." The teaching of Jesus was therefore prophetic in character, resulting from direct inspiration, and was not based upon tradition like that of the Pharisees. In this respect He was in line with the Teacher of Righteousness of the Qumrān sect "to whom God has made known all the mysteries of the words of his servants, the prophets" (1QpHab, VII, 4–5). The interpretation of the prophets' words was a direct revelation from God to the Teacher of Righteousness, and he was the source of Biblical interpretation for the community.

The teaching of Jesus elucidates an interesting passage in 1QS, V, 25, to VI, 1: "One shall not speak to his brother [according to emendation of the text] in anger or in complaint or with a (stiff) neck, or . . . a wicked spirit; nor shall he hate him . . . of his heart, though he shall reprove him on the very day so as not to incur guilt because of him. And also let not a man bring accusation against his neighbor in the presence of the many who has not been subject to (previous) reproof before witnesses."

According to this passage there is first a personal reproof of an erring brother, then a reproof before witnesses, and finally, a reproof before the whole group or community. So Jesus, in Matt. 18:15–17, specifies three stages in dealing with an erring brother: "Moreover, if thy brother shall trespass against thee, go and tell

[16] Dupont-Sommer, *The Jewish Sect of Qumrân and the Essenes*, especially pp. 147–166.

him his fault between thee and him alone: if he shall hear thee, thou hast gained thy brother. But if he will not hear thee, then take with thee one or more, that in the mouth of two or three witnesses every word may be established. And if he shall neglect to hear them, tell it unto the church: but if he neglect to hear the church, let him be unto thee as an heathen man and a publican."

1QS, VIII, 1, describes the Council of the Community,[17] composed of nine laymen and three priests. The members of this inner conclave—perhaps the *sōd* of 1QS, VI, 19—exemplified in a special way the perfect life of devotion to the Torah. Although their exact duties and powers are not given, they must have served as a Supreme Court, collaborating with the head of the community in the direction of the sect. As a group, they suggest the twelve disciples whom Jesus gathered to receive special instruction and to carry on His work after his death.

The Messianic teachings of the Essene Covenanters are particularly interesting because of their relation to the work and teachings of Jesus. In a valuable series of articles in the *United Presbyterian,* Professor Brownlee has shown how strongly the Servant Songs of Second Isaiah influenced the Messianic thinking of the Qumrān sect.[18] For instance, a new reading of a difficult form in Is. 52:14, which has been found in 1QIs[a], seems to indicate that the sect identified the Suffering Servant with the Messiah. For the difficult form, *mšḥt,* usually translated "marred," 1QIs[a] has *mšḥty,* which is probably to be translated "I have anointed." [19] The verse, according to 1QIs[a], would then read: "As many were astonished at you; so I anointed his appearance above any man, and his form above any of the sons of man." It would seem, therefore, that the textual tradition of 1QIs[a] from Qumrān reflects a Messianic interpretation of the Servant in Is. 52:13–53:12.

Another Messianic passage in 1QS (VIII, 4–7) describes the

[17] See p. 63.
[18] W. H. Brownlee, "The Cross of Christ in the Light of Ancient Scrolls," *UP,* Nov. 30, Dec. 7, 14, 21, and 28, 1953.
[19] See W. H. Brownlee, "The Servant of the Lord in the Qumrān Scrolls," Pt. I, *BASOR,* No. 132, Dec., 1953, 10–12, and others.

sect as the embodiment of the Servant ideal. The Council of twelve men, just mentioned, are "to expiate iniquity through deeds of justice and through the hardship of refining," and through their perfect administration of the affairs of the sect to bring about the Messianic Age:

When these things come to pass in Israel, the Council of the Community will have been established in truth: for an eternal planting, a holy house for Israel, a holy of holies for Aaron, true witnesses regarding religion, and the chosen of divine acceptance to atone for the earth, and to render to the wicked their desert.

According to these words the community fulfills the mission of the Servant by witnessing to the religion (*mišpaṭ*) of Yahweh, by making atonement for the earth, and rendering punishment to the wicked.[20] In this way the Messianic Age will be ushered in when God's eternal ordinances will be established, and wickedness will be destroyed.

Still another passage in 1QS (IV, 20–22) assumes Messianic importance in the light of the Servant Songs of Second Isaiah. Stating that God has appointed a time when perversity shall end and universal truth shall prevail, it goes on:

And then God will purify by His truth all the deeds of a man; and He will refine him more than the sons of man, in order to consume every evil spirit from the midst of his flesh, and to cleanse him with the Holy Spirit from all deeds of wickedness; and He will sprinkle upon him the spirit of truth as purifying water (to cleanse him) from all abominations of falsehood and from being contaminated with the spirit of impurity, so that he may instruct the upright in the knowledge of the Most High and the wisdom of the sons of heaven, in order to make wise the perfect of the way.

"He will refine him more than the sons of man" describes the sufferings of the Messiah in terms like those of Is. 52:14. God "will sprinkle upon him the spirit of truth," so that he in turn may "sprinkle many nations" (Is. 52:15).[21] Through the suffering of

[20] Cf. Is. 42:1–4 and 53:1–12.
[21] See p. 115, n. 6.

the Messiah comes knowledge (cf. Is. 53:11), whereby He makes "wise the perfect of the way" (cf. Is. 52:13 and Dan. 12:3). 1QS then states that "God has chosen" the community "to be an eternal covenant" (IV, 22), just as in the Servant Songs, the Servant himself becomes the covenant, or the embodiment of the covenant, in whom God and His people are eternally united (Is. 42:6, 49:8).

These passages make clear that the Servant ideal was interpreted in a corporate as well as an individual sense by the Qumrān sect, just as in the Servant Songs of Isaiah. God, at the time of His visitation, will send a man—the Messiah—who will fulfill all the ideals of the Covenant Community, and who, like the Community, will make atonement for the world through his suffering. Thus before the time of Christ the Messianic concept was joined with the Suffering Servant ideal in the Jewish Covenanter sect of Qumrān. The way was now theologically prepared for the coming of God's Son, in whom the Messianic hopes of Israel were to be fulfilled and the mission of the Servant realized.

These profound Messianic teachings of the Essenes must have been known by Jesus. There is little doubt that His own Messianic consciousness was strongly influenced by their interpretation of the Old Testament Prophets.[22]

The Last Supper

The rites and theological significance of the Essene communal meal are exceedingly important for an understanding of the origins of the Lord's Supper in the New Testament.[23] Josephus gives a rather full account of the rites connected with the communal meal of the Essenes.[24] He states that the members bathed their bodies

---

[22] On the eschatology of the Qumrān sect, cf. also: W. H. Brownlee, "The Servant of the Lord in the Qumrân Scrolls," Pt. II, BASOR, No. 135, Oct., 1954, 33–38; M. Delcor, "L'Éschatologie des documents de Khirbet Qumrān," RSR, XCIV (1952), 363–386; H. L. Ginsberg, "The Oldest Interpretation of the Suffering Servant," VT, III (1953), 400–404.

[23] Four accounts of the institution of the Lord's Supper are given in the New Testament: Matt. 26:26–29, Mk. 14:22–25, Lk. 22:19–20, and I Cor. 11:19–20.

[24] WJ, II, viii, 5.

with cold water, then clothed themselves in white robes, entered the dining room as a holy temple and quietly took their accustomed places. When the food was set before them, and the priest had said grace over it, they ate. Then the priest again said grace. Thus at the beginning and end of the meal they praised God for the blessings He had bestowed upon them. This ceremony was repeated twice a day, at the noon and evening meals.

To this ritual the Manual of the Qumrān sect adds several significant points. One regulation of the community was that "they shall eat communally, and bless communally, and take counsel communally" (1QS, VI, 2–3). The fact that the members were to eat and bless communally shows that the meal was sacramental in character. This is emphasized by the priestly blessing of the bread and wine: "And it shall be when they arrange the table to eat, or the wine to drink, the priest shall stretch forth his hand first to bless with the first fruits of the bread and the wine" (1QS, VI, 4–5, omitting dittography in the original text). Furthermore, this communal meal was Messianic in character, because the "Messiah of Israel" was considered to be present.[25]

Professor K. G. Kuhn, of the University of Göttingen, has recently shown that the Essene communal meal, as described by Josephus and the newly discovered Manual, throws light upon the origins and meaning of the Christian Sacrament of the Lord's Supper.[26] The fact that Peter beckoned to John "that he [i.e., John] should ask who it should be of whom he spake" (John 13:24), may now be understood in the light of the practice of the Qumrān community when they met together in sessions: "Not shall a man speak in the midst of the words of his neighbor, before his brother finishes speaking. Neither shall he speak before his proper order" (1QS, VI, 10). Evidently John, who sat next to Jesus (cf. John 13:25), held a higher rank in the group than Peter, and was the one to address the question to Jesus. More important

[25] See p. 32.
[26] "Über den ursprünglichen Sinn des Abendmahles und sein Verhältnis zu den Gemeinschaftsmahlen der Sektenschrift," ET, X (1950), 508–527.

are the actual parallels between the Essene communal meal and the Lord's Supper of the New Testament. In both cases only men participated. In both groups the recognized leader presided over the meal. Finally, the leader blessed both the bread and the wine. Because of these close parallels, Professor Kuhn believes that the background of the Lord's Supper must be sought in the communal meal of an Essenian group like the Qumrān sect, rather than in the Passover meal, which is definitely a family rite over which the father of the family presides.

The Book of Acts

The idea of "community," as we have noted so frequently, penetrated the whole life of the Qumrān sect. "All members shall be in true community and good humility and loyal love and zeal for righteousness, each toward his friend in the holy council and as sons of the holy conclave" (1QS, II, 24–25). This sharing of the spiritual life among the members of the community went hand in hand with daily communal living. Not only did these Essenes eat together, but they turned over their wealth and wages to the Supervisor of the community who had charge of the general treasury.[27]

This idea of communal living, found in the Qumrān Essene community, is strikingly similar to the communal life which, according to the Book of Acts, was practiced in the early Church. "And all that believed were together, and had all things in common; and sold their possessions and goods, and parted them to all men, as every man had need. And they, continuing daily with one accord in the temple, and breaking bread from house to house, did eat their meat with gladness and singleness of heart, praising God, and having favor with all the people" (Acts 2:44–47). Also: "And the multitude of them that believed were of one heart and of one soul: neither said any of them that ought of the things which he possessed was his own; but they all had things in common" (Acts 4:32). Thus, in spiritual as well as practical matters,

[27] See p. 65.

the members of the early Church, like the Essenes, had all things in common.

Paul

Many of the terms and ideas in the Pauline literature are closely paralleled in the sectarian documents from Qumrān. For the first time, for instance, we have the Hebrew equivalents of such New Testament Greek expressions as "body of flesh" (Col. 1:22 and 1QpHab, IX, 3), and "flesh of sin" (Rom. 8:3 and 1QS, XI, 9, and 1QM, IV, 3).

The decisions of the Qumrān community were made in accordance with the judgment of the many. This idea is expressed by the phrase "at their mouth the decision of the lot comes forth concerning every matter" (1QS, V, 3—cf. also VI, 16). Although the decisions of the community were not made by actually casting lots, but rather by determining the majority opinion, the word "lot" no doubt retained the connotation of the divine will or purpose which was made manifest in the decision.[28] Those who did not belong to the Covenant sect were called "the men of Belial's lot" (1QS, II, 5), whereas the Covenanters themselves were called "the men of God's Lot" (1QS, II, 2), that is, the people of God's choosing (cf. Eph. 1:18, 5:5). The "eternal lot" (1QH, III, 22) reminds us of the expression *aiōnios klēronomia* found in Heb. 9:15.[29]

The members of the Qumrān sect believed that they had been called to wage eternal warfare against the forces of Belial. This military aspect of the Community's spiritual life, so clearly brought out in the War Scroll, reminds one of the passages in the New

---

[28] Cf. Acts 1:24–26, which describes the choice of Matthias by lot to fill the place of Judas. Notice that the Christian community first prayed that the Lord would show which of the two men—Joseph or Matthias—He had selected. The decision reached by casting lots was therefore the manifestation of the divine will.

[29] Professor K. G. Kuhn has discussed the significance of many terms in the Qumrān sectarian documents for New Testament studies in two excellent articles: "Die in Palästina gefundenen hebräischen Texte und das Neue Testament," ZTK, XLVII (1950), 192–211, and "*Peirasmos hamartia—sarx* im Neuen Testament und die damit zusammenhängenden Vorstellungen," ZTK, XLIX (1952), 200–222.

Testament which describe the Christian life as a struggle against the forces of darkness and evil. In Rom. 13:12–14, for instance, we read: "The night is far spent, the day is at hand: let us therefore cast off the works of darkness, and let us put on the armor of light. Let us walk honestly as in the day; not in rioting and drunkenness, not in chambering and wantonness, not in strife and envying. But put ye on the Lord Jesus Christ, and make not provision for the flesh, to fulfill the lusts thereof." And Paul's description of the Christian's armor in Eph. 6:11–17, which is deeply rooted in this tradition, reads as follows: "Put on the whole armor of God, that ye may be able to stand against the wiles of the devil. For we wrestle not against flesh and blood, but against principalities, against powers, against the rulers of the darkness of this world, against spiritual wickedness in high places. Wherefore take unto you the whole armor of God, that ye may be able to withstand in the evil day, and having done all to stand. Stand therefore, having your loins girt about with truth, and having on the breastplate of righteousness; and your feet shod with the preparation of the gospel of peace; above all, taking the shield of faith, wherewith ye shall be able to quench all the fiery darts of the wicked. And take the helmet of salvation, and the sword of the Spirit, which is the word of God."

But most striking of all is the similarity between the Pauline doctrine of justification by faith, and that which is found in the Qumrān sectarian documents. In one of the Hymns, for instance, we read: "Not to man is righteousness, and not to the son of man is the perfection of way, but to God Most High belong deeds of righteousness" (1QH, IV, 30–31). But this doctrine is expressed most clearly in the last column of 1QS: "For as for me, my justification [*mišpaṭ*] belongs to God, and in His hand is the perfection of my way with the uprightness of my heart. And in His righteousness my transgression is blotted out. . . . And in His mercy He has brought me near, and in His loving kindness He brings my justification [*mišpaṭ*]. In His faithful righteousness He has justified me, and in the bounty of His goodness He pardons all my iniquities, and in His righteousness He cleanses me from the impurity of man and the sin of the children of men" (XI, 2–3, 13–15). We find here not only the rudiments of Paul's doctrine of justification by faith—apart from Christ, of course—as expressed in Romans 3 and Gal. 2 and 3, but also the doctrine of sanctification.[30]

With these passages must be included the interpretation in 1QpHab (VIII, 1–3), of the famous verse Hab. 2:4 to mean that "God will deliver from the house of judgment" all the doers of the law "for the sake of their labor and their faith in the Teacher of Righteousness." Here the writer, like Paul, interprets *'emūnah* in the sense of a personal faith which brings salvation.[31]

---

[30] Cf. also 1QH, IV, 37.

[31] Several articles, not mentioned in this chapter, which discuss the relation of the Qumrān documents to the New Testament, may be cited here: W. Grossouw, "The Dead Sea Scrolls and the New Testament," SC, XXVI (1951), 289–299, and XXVII (1952), 1–8. G. Vermès, "Le 'Commentaire d'Habacuc' et le Nouveau Testament," CS, V (1951), 337–349. W. D. Davies, " 'Knowledge' in the Dead Sea Scrolls and Matthew 11:25–30," HTR, XLVI (1953), 113–139. C. G. Howie, "The Cosmic Struggle," Interpretation, VIII (1954), 206–217. L. Mowry, "The Dead Sea Scrolls and the Background for the Gospel of John," BA, XVII (1954), 78–97. F. M. Braun, "L'Arrière-fond judaïque du quatrième évangile et la Communauté de l'Alliance," RB, LXII (1955), 5–44. R. E. Brown, "The Qumrān Scrolls and the Johannine Gospel and Epistles," CBQ, XVII (1955), 403–419. B. Gärtner, "The Habakkuk Commentary (DSH) and the Gospel of Matthew," ST, VIII (1955), 1–24.

Abbreviations

1QS	Manual of Discipline
1QpHab	Habakkuk Commentary
1QH	Thanksgiving Hymns
1QM	War Scroll
1QIs^a	Isaiah Scroll (published by the American Schools of Oriental Research)
1QIs^b	Isaiah Scroll (published by E. L. Sukenik, Hebrew University)
CDC	Cairo Genizah Document of the Damascus Covenanters
AV	Authorized Version
M	Masoretic Text
LXX	Septuagint
AJ	*Antiquities of the Jews*
AO	*Archiv Orientálni*
BA	*Biblical Archaeologist*
BASOR	*Bulletin of the American Schools of Oriental Research*
Bib.	*Biblica*
BJRL	*Bulletin of the John Rylands Library*
BO	*Bibliotheca Orientalis*
CBQ	*Catholic Biblical Quarterly*
CC	*Christian Century*
CQ	*Congregational Quarterly*
CS	*Cahiers Sioniens*
DTT	*Dansk Teologisk Tidsskrift*
DV	*Dieu Vivant*
ET	*Evangelische Theologie*
ETL	*Ephemerides Theologicae Lovanienses*
Ex.T	*Expository Times*
HDB	James Hastings' *Dictionary of the Bible*
HTR	*Harvard Theological Review*
HUCA	*Hebrew Union College Annual*
IEJ	*Israel Exploration Journal*

IKT	*Internationale Kirchliche Zeitschrift*
Int.	*Interpretation*
ITQ	*Irish Theological Quarterly*
JBL	*Journal of Biblical Literature*
JJS	*Journal of Jewish Studies*
JNES	*Journal of Near Eastern Studies*
JPOS	*Journal of the Palestine Oriental Society*
JQR	*Jewish Quarterly Review*
LV	*Lumière et Vie*
MC	*Modern Churchman*
MSR	*Mélanges de Science Religieuse*
NC	*La Nouvelle Clio*
NRT	*Nouvelle Revue Théologique*
NTS	*New Testament Studies*
OM	*Oriente Moderno*
OS	*Oudtestamentische Studiën*
PEQ	*Palestine Exploration Quarterly*
PJB	*Palästinajahrbuch*
RB	*Revue Biblique*
RBI	*Rivista Biblica Italiana*
RE	*Review and Expositor*
REB	*Revista Eclesiástica Brasileira*
RHPR	*Revue d'Histoire et de Philosophie Religieuses*
RHR	*Revue de l'Histoire des Religions*
RSPT	*Revue des Sciences Philosophiques et Théologiques*
RSR	*Recherches de Science Religieuse*
SC	*Studia Catholica*
Scr.	*Scripture*
Sef.	*Sefarad*
SKZ	*Schweizerische Kirchen-Zeitung*
ST	*Studia Theologica*
STK	*Svensk Teologisk Kvartalskrift*
STU	*Schweizer Theologische Umschau*
SZ	*Stimmen der Zeit*
TLZ	*Theologische Literaturzeitung*
TrierZ	*Trierer Zeitschrift*
TTK	*Tidsskrift for Teologi og Kirke*
TZ	*Theologische Zeitschrift*
UP	*United Presbyterian*
VT	*Vetus Testamentum*
VV	*Verdad y Vida*

WJ	*Wars of the Jews*
ZAW	*Zeitschrift für die alttestamentliche Wissenschaft*
ZKT	*Zeitschrift für katholische Theologie*
ZRG	*Zeitschrift für Religions—und Geistesgeschichte*
ZTK	*Zeitschrift für Theologie und Kirche*

Bibliography

This list includes most of the articles and books on the Dead Sea Scrolls and related subjects that have appeared from 1953 to the summer of 1955. I have consulted most of them. However, a few appeared too late to be used.

Abramson, S., and H. L. Ginsberg, "On the Aramaic Deed of Sale of the Third Year of the Second Jewish Revolt," *BASOR*, No. 136, Dec., 1954, 17–19.

Allegro, J. M., "A Newly Discovered Fragment of a Commentary on Ps. XXXVII from Qumrân," *PEQ*, LXXXVI (1954), 69–75

————,"Some Archaeological Sites and the Old Testament: Qumrân," *Ex.T*, LXVI (1955), 259–262.

Arnaldich, L., "La Alianza con Dios, ideal de la restauracíon del orden religioso destruido según la secta del Mar Muerto," *35 Congreso Eucarístico Internacional 1952: Sesiones de Estudio*, I (Barcelona, 1954), 341–344.

————, "El Supuesto Christo del Mar Mortuo," *VV*, XI (1953). 57–71.

Audet, J. P., "Affinités littéraires et doctrinales du Manuel de discipline," *RB*, LX (1953), 41–82.

Baillet, M., "Fragments araméens de Qumrân: Description de la Jérusalem Nouvelle," *RB*, LXII (1955), 222–245.

Bardtke, H., "Bemerkungen zu den beiden Texten aus dem Bar-Kochba-Aufstand," *TLZ*, LXXIX (1954), 295–304.

————, *Die Handschriftenfunde am Toten Meer*, 2nd ed. Berlin, 1953.

————, "Die Parascheneinteilung der Jesaiarolle I von Qumran," *Festschrift Franz Dornseiff* (Leipzig, 1954), 32–75.

Barthélemy, D., "Redécouverte d'un chaînon manquant de l'histoire de la Septante," *RB*, LX (1953), 18–29.

————, J. T. Milik, et al., *Qumran Cave*, Vol. I (1st vol. in *Discoveries in the Judaean Desert*). Oxford: Clarendon Press, 1955.

Baumgärtel, D. F., "Zur Liturgie in der 'Sektenrolle' vom Toten Meer," ZAW, LXVI (1953), 263–265.

Baumgarten, J. M., "Sacrifice and Worship Among the Jewish Sectarians of the Dead Sea (Qumrân) Scrolls," HTR, XLVI (1953), 141–159.

———, and M. Mansoor, "Studies in the New Hodayot (Thanksgiving Hymns)," JBL, LXXIV (1955), 115–124, 188–195.

Baumgartner, W., "Die Bedeutung der Höhlenfunde aus Palästina für die Theologie," STU, XXIV (1954), 49–63.

———, "Neues von den palästinischen Handschriftenfunden," TZ, IX (1953), 315–318, 469–473.

Bea, A., "Neue Handschriftenfunde in Palästina," SZ, CLII (1953), 248–253.

Beegle, D. M., "Ligatures with Waw and Yodh in the Dead Sea Scrolls," BASOR, No. 129, Feb., 1953, 11–14.

Birnbaum, S. A., "Bar Kokhba and Akiba," PEQ, LXXXVI (1954), 23–32.

———, "The Beth Mashku Document," PEQ, LXXXVI (1955), 21–33.

———, "An Unknown Aramaic Cursive (from Murabba'at)," PEQ, LXXXV (1953), 23–41.

Bonsirven, J., La Bible apocryphe: En marge de l'Ancien Testament. Paris: A. Fayard, 1953.

Braun, F. M., "L'Arrière-fond judaïque du quatrième évangile et la Communauté de l'Alliance," RB, LXII (1955), 5–44.

Brown, R. E., "The Qumrân Scrolls and the Johannine Gospel and Epistles," CBQ, XVII (1955), 403–419.

Brownlee, W. H., "The Cross of Christ in the Light of Ancient Scrolls," UP, Nov. 30, Dec. 7, 14, 21, and 28, 1953.

———, "Emendations of the Dead Sea Manual of Discipline and Some Notes Concerning the Habakkuk Midrash," JQR, XLV (1954), 141–158, 198–218.

———, "In the Light of Ancient Scrolls: 'Salvation,' a Messianic Title in Jewish Books," UP, Dec. 6, 1954.

———, "The Incarnation in the Light of Ancient Scrolls," UP, Jan. 31, 1955.

———, "John the Baptist in the New Light of Ancient Scrolls," Int., IX (1955), 71–90.

———, "The Servant of the Lord in the Qumrân Scrolls," Pt. I, BASOR, No. 132, Dec., 1953, 8–15; ibid., Pt. II, No. 135, Oct., 1954, 33–38.

Carmignac, J., "Les Kittim dans la 'Guerre des fils de lumière contre les fils de ténèbres,'" *NRT*, LXXVII (1955), 737–748.

Chamberlain, J. V., "Another Qumran Thanksgiving Psalm," *JNES*, XIV (1955), 32–41.

——, "Further Elucidation of a Messianic Thanksgiving Psalm from Qumran," *JNES*, XIV (1955), 181–182.

Considine, J. S., "The Dead Sea Scrolls," *CBQ*, XVI (1954), 41–45.

Coppens, J., *Les Documents du Désert de Juda et les origines du Christianisme* (ALBO, Ser. II, fasc. 39), Louvain, 1953.

——, "Où en est le problème des manuscrits de Qumrān?" *NC*, VI (1954), 247–257.

——, "La Secte de Qumrān et son attente eschatologique," *NC*, V (1953), 5–9.

Couroyer, B., "A propos de dépôts de manuscrits dans des jarres," *RB*, LXII (1955), 76–81.

Cross, F. M., Jr., "The Essenes and Their Master," *CC*, Aug. 17, 1955.

——, "The Manuscripts of the Dead Sea Caves," *BA*, XVII (1954), 1–21.

——, "A New Qumran Biblical Fragment Related to the Original Hebrew Underlying the Septuagint," *BASOR*, No. 132, Dec., 1953, 15–26.

——, "The Oldest Manuscripts from Qumran," *JBL*, LXXIV (1955), 147–172.

——, "The Scrolls and the New Testament," *CC*, Aug. 24, 1955.

——, "The Scrolls and the Old Testament," *CC*, Aug. 10, 1955.

——, "The Scrolls from the Judean Wilderness," *CC*, Aug. 3, 1955.

Cullmann, O., "Die neuentdeckten Qumrantexte und das Judenchristentum der Pseudoklementinen," *Neutestamentliche Studien für Rudolf Bultmann* (BZNW, No. 21—Berlin, A. Topelmann, 1954), 35–51.

Daniélou, J., "La Communauté de Qumrān et l'organisation de l'Eglise ancienne," *RHPR*, XXXV (1955), 104–116.

——, "Une Source de la Spiritualité chrétienne dans les manuscrits de la Mer morte: La Doctrine de deux esprits," *DV*, XXV (1953), 127–136.

Davies, W. D., " 'Knowledge' in the Dead Sea Scrolls and Matthew 11: 25–30," *HTR*, XLVI (1953), 113–139.

Decroix, J., "Les Manuscrits de la Mer morte: Essai de bibliographie," *MSR*, X (1953), 107–124.

Delcor, M., "Contribution à l'étude de la législation des sectaires de Damas et de Qumrân," *RB*, LXI (1954), 533–553, LXII (1955), 60–75.

——, "Des diverses manières d'écrire le tétragramme sacré dans les anciens documents hébraïques," *RHR*, CXLVII (1955), 145–173.

——, "La Guerre des fils de lumière contre les fils de ténèbres," *NRT*, LXXVII (1955), 372–399.

——, "L'Immortalité de l'âme dans le Livre de la Sagesse et dans les documents de Qumrân," *NRT*, LXXVII (1955), 614–630.

——, "Le Sacerdoce, les lieux de culte, les rites et les fêtes dans les documents de Khirbet Qumrân," *RHR*, XCLV (1953), 5–41.

Detaye, C., "Le Cadre historique du Midrash d'Habacuc," *ETL*, XXX (1954), 323–343.

Driver, G. R., "Once Again the Judaean Scrolls," *JQR*, XLIV (1953), 1–20.

Dubarle, A. M., "Une Source du Livre de la Sagesse?" *RSPT*, XXXVII (1953), 425–443.

Dupont-Sommer, A., "Le Couvent essénien du Désert de Juda," *Revue de Paris*, LXI (1954), 101–114.

——, *The Jewish Sect of Qumrân and the Essenes*, transl. (of *Nouveaux aperçus*, following) by R. D. Barnett. London: Vallentine, Mitchell & Co., 1954; New York: Macmillan Co., 1955.

——, "La Mère du Messie et la mère de l'Aspic dans un hymne de Qoumrān," *RHR*, CXLVII (1955), 174–188.

——, *Nouveaux aperçus sur les manuscrits de la Mer morte* (L'Orient ancien illustré, No. 5). Paris: Adrien Maisonneuve, 1953.

——, "Le Problème des influences étrangères sur la secte juive de Qoumrān," *RHPR*, XXXV (1955), 75–94.

——, "Quelques remarques sur le *Commentaire d'Habacuc* à propos d'un livre récent," *VT*, V (1955), 113–129.

Elliger, K., *Studien zum Habakuk-Kommentar vom Toten Meer* (Beiträge zur historischen Theologie, No. 15). Tübingen, 1953.

Erbetta, M., "Presso il Mar morto, alla vigilia del Precursore," *Euntes Docete*, VII (1954), 103–109.

Flusser, D., "The Apocryphal Book of *Ascensio Isaiae* and the Dead Sea Sect," *IEJ*, III (1953), 30–47.

Fritsch, C. T., "Herod the Great and the Qumran Community," *JBL*, LXXIV (1955), 173–181.

Gärtner, B., "The Habakkuk Commentary (DSH) and the Gospel of Matthew," *ST*, VIII (1955), 1–24.

Ginsberg, H. L., "Notes on the Two Published Letters to Jeshua ben Galgolah," *BASOR*, No. 131, Oct., 1953, 25–27.

——, "The Oldest Interpretation of the Suffering Servant," *VT*, III (1953), 400–404.

Goossens, R., "L'Enigme du signe 'nun' dans le Manuel de discipline," *NC*, VI (1954), 5–39.

Gottstein, M. H., "Anti-Essene Traits in the DSS," *VT*, IV (1954), 141–147.

——, "Bemerkungen zu Eissfeldt's variae lectiones der Jesaiah-Rolle," *Bib.*, XXXIV (1953), 212–221.

——, "Biblical Quotations in the Dead Sea Scrolls," *VT*, III (1953), 79–82.

——, "A DSS Biblical Variant in a Medieval Treatise," *VT*, III (1953), 187–188.

——, "Die Jesaiah-Rolle im Lichte von Peschitta und Targum," *Bib.*, XXXV (1954), 51–71.

——, "Die Jesaiah-Rolle und das Problem der hebräischen Bibel-handschriften," *Bib.*, XXXV (1954), 429–442.

——, "Studies in the Language of the DSS," *JJS*, IV (1953), 104–107.

——, "A Supposed Dittography in DSD," *VT*, IV (1954), 422–424.

Graystone, G., "The Dead Sea Scrolls," *Scr.*, V (1953), 112–122, VI (1953), 17–21, VI (1954), 131–143, VII (1955), 66–75.

——, "The Dead Sea Scrolls and the New Testament," *ITQ*, XXII (1955).

Hammershaimb, E., "Håndskriftfundene fra egnene ved Det doede hav," *DTT*, XVII (1954), 65–79.

Harding, G. L., "Notes and News," *Annual of the Department of Antiquities of Jordan*, II (1953), 5–7, 82–85, 90.

Hempel, J., "Die Funde in der Wüste," *Almanach auf das Jahr des Herrn 1954*, 69–81.

Honeyman, A. M., "Notes on a Teacher and a Book," *JJS*, IV (1953), 131–132.

Howie, C. G., "The Cosmic Struggle," *Int.*, VIII (1954), 206–217.

Jaubert, A., "Le Calendrier des Jubilés et de la secte de Qumrān: Ses origines bibliques," *VT*, III (1953), 250–264.

Johnson, S. E., "The Dead Sea Manual and the Jerusalem Church of Acts," *ZAW*, LXVI (1954), 106–120.

Jungmann, J. A., "Altchristliche Gebetsordnung im Lichte des Regelbuches von 'En Fešcha," *ZKT*, LXXV (1953), 215–219.

Junker, H., "Neues Licht über die biblische Text- und Zeitgeschichte," *TrierZ*, LXIII (1954), 65–76.

Kahle, P., "Die im August 1952 entdeckte Lederrolle mit dem griechischen Text der Kleinen Propheten und das Problem der Septuaginta," *TLZ*, LXXIX (1954), col. 81–94.

——, "The Karaites and the Manuscripts from the Cave," *VT*, III (1953), 82–84.

Kelso, J. L., "The Archeology of Qumran," *JBL*, LXXIV (1955), 141–146.

Kipper, B., "Novedades exegéticas," *REB*, XIII (1953), 928–932.

Kuhn, K. G., "Die beiden Messias Aarons und Israels," *NTS*, I (1954), 168–179.

——, "Les Rouleaux de cuivre de Qumran," *RB*, LXI (1954), 193–205.

Lacheman, E. R., "Hebrew Paleography Again," *JQR*, XLIV (1953), 116–122.

——, "The So-Called Bar Kokba Letter," *JQR*, XLIV (1953), 285–290.

van 't Land, F. A. W., and A. S. van der Woude, *De Habakuk-rol van 'Ain Fašha*. Assen, 1954.

Laridon, V., "Nieuwe archeologische en literaire vondsten in de Woestijn van Juda," *Coll. Brugenses*, XLIX (1953), 458–468.

Lehmann, O. H., "A Third Dead Sea Scroll of Isaiah," *JJS*, IV (1953), 38–40.

——, and S. M. Stern, "A Legal Certificate from Bar Kochba's Days," *VT*, III (1953), 391–396.

Lemoine, F. M., "Les Manuscrits du Désert de Juda," *LV*, VIII (1953), 110–126.

Lindblom, J., "Nya Handskriftsfynd i Främre Orienten," *STK*, XXX (1954), 1–9.

Loewinger, S., "The Variants of DSI II," *VT*, IV (1954), 155–163.

Mantey, J. R., "Baptism in the DS Manual of Discipline," *RE*, LI (1954), 522–527.

Marcus, R., "A Note on the Bar Kokeba Letter from Murabba'at," *JNES*, XIII (1954), 51.

——, "Pharisees, Essenes and Gnostics," *JBL*, LXXIII (1954), 157–161.

Michaud, H., "Un Mythe zervanite dans un des manuscrits de Qumrān," *VT*, V (1955), 137–147.

——, "A propos du nom de Qumrān," *RHPR*, XXXV (1955), 68–74.

Michel, A., *Le Maître de justice.* Avignon, 1954.

Mikasnomiya, Prince, "Notes on Some Hebraic Texts Found in the Caves of Murabba'at," *Paleologia* (Osaka, 1954), III, 159–168.

Milik, J. T., "Un Contrat juif de l'an 134 après J.-C.," *RB,* LXI (1954), 182–190.

―――, "Une Inscription et une lettre en araméen Christo-palestinien," *RB,* LX (1953), 526–539.

―――, "Une Lettre de Siméon bar Kokheba," *RB,* LX (1953), 276–294.

―――, "Note additionnelle sur le contrat juif de l'an 134 après Jésus-Christ," *RB,* LXII (1955), 253–254.

―――, "Le Testament de Lévi en araméen: Fragment de la grotte 4 de Qumrān," *RB,* LXII (1955), 398–406.

―――, "Trois ans de travail aux manuscrits du Désert de Juda," *Antemurale* (Rome, 1954), I, 113–140.

Moe, Olaf, "Handskriftfunnene ved det Doede Hav," *TTK,* XXV (1954), 8–17.

Molin, G., "Hat die Sekte von Khirbet Qumrān Beziehungen zu Aegypten?" *TLZ,* LXXVIII (1953), col. 653–656.

―――, *Die Söhne des Lichtes: Zeit und Stellung der Handschriften vom Toten Meer.* Wien, 1954.

Moscati, S., "I Manoscritti ebraici del Deserto di Giuda," *OM,* XXXIV, (1954), 438–452, 505–521, 566–575.

Mowry, L., "The Dead Sea Scrolls and the Background for the Gospel of John," *BA,* XVII (1954), 78–97.

Muilenburg, J., "Fragments of Another Qumran Isaiah Scroll" and "A Qoheleth Scroll from Qumran," *BASOR,* No. 135, Oct., 1954, 28–32, 20–28.

North, R., "The Damascus of Qumrân Geography," *PEQ,* LXXXVI (1955), 34–48.

―――, "Qumrân and Its Archeology," *CBQ,* XVI (1954), 426–437.

―――, "The Qumrân 'Sadducees,'" *CBQ,* XVII (1955), 164–188.

Nötscher, F., "'Gesetz der Freiheit' im NT und in der Monchsgemeinde am Toten Meer," *Bib.,* XXXIV (1953), 193–194.

Orlinsky, H. M., "Studies in the St. Mark's Scroll V," *IEJ,* IV (1954), 5–8.

Otzen, B., "Die neugefundenen hebräischen Sektenschriften und die Testamente der zwölf Patriarchen," *ST,* VII (1954), 125–157.

Parrot, A., "Les Manuscrits de la Mer morte: Le Point de vue archéologique," *RHPR*, XXXV (1955), 61–67.

van der Ploeg, J., "Les Manuscrits du Désert de Juda," *BO*, XI (1954), 145–160.

Rabin, C., "Notes on the Habakkuk Scroll and the Zadokite Document," *VT*, V (1955), 148–162.

————, *The Zadokite Documents*. Oxford: Clarendon Press, 1954.

Rabinowitz, I., "A Hebrew Letter of the Second Century from Beth Mashko," *BASOR*, No. 131, Oct., 1953, 21–24.

————, "A Reconsideration of 'Damascus' and '390 Years' in the 'Damascus' ('Zadokite') Fragments," *JBL*, LXXIII (1954), 11–35.

————, "Sequence and Dates of the Extra-Biblical Dead Sea Scroll Texts and 'Damascus' Fragments," *VT*, III (1953), 175–185.

Rabinowitz, J. J., "The Legal Document from Murabba'at," *Bib.*, XXXV, (1954), 198–206.

————, "Note sur la lettre de Bar Kokheba," *RB*, LXI (1954), 191–192.

————, "Some Notes on an Aramaic Contract from the Dead Sea Region," *BASOR*, No. 136, Dec., 1954, 15–16.

Reed, W. L., "The Qumrân Caves Expedition of March, 1952," *BASOR*, No. 135, Oct., 1954, 8–13.

Reicke, B., "Traces of Gnosticism in the Dead Sea Scrolls?" *NTS*, I (1954), 137–141.

————, "Die Verfassung der Urgemeinde im Lichte jüdischer Dokumente," *TZ*, X (1954), 95–112.

Reider, J., and W. H. Brownlee, "On MŠḤTY in the Qumrân Scrolls," *BASOR*, No. 134, Apr., 1954, 27–28.

Roberts, B. J., "The Dead Sea Scrolls and the Old Testament Scriptures," *BJRL*, XXXVI (1953), 75–96.

————, "The Qumrân Scrolls: A Survey," *CQ*, XXXII (1954), 114–124.

Rolla, A., "Manoscritti ebraici del deserto di Giuda," *RBI*, I (1953), 116–135.

Rost, L., "Der 'Lehrer der Einung' und der 'Lehrer der Gerechtigkeit,' " *TLZ*, LXXVIII (1953), col. 143–148.

————, "Zum 'Buch der Kriege der Söhne des Lichts gegen die Söhne der Finsternis,' " *TLZ*, LXXX (1955), col. 205–208.

Rowley, H. H., *The Dead Sea Scrolls and Their Significance*. London: Independent Press, 1955.

Rubinstein, A., "The Appellation 'Galileans' in Ben Kosebha's Letter to Ben Galgola," *JJS*, VI (1955), 26–34.

———, "Formal Agreement of Parallel Clauses in the Isaiah Scroll," *VT*, IV (1954), 316–321.

———, "Isaiah 52:14—MŠHT—and the DSIa Variant," *Bib.*, XXXV (1954), 475–479.

———, "Isaiah 52:14—MSHT—and the DSIa Variant," *Bib.*, (1954), 200–201.

———, "Notes on the Use of the Tenses in the Variant Readings of the Isaiah Scroll," *VT*, III (1953), 92–95.

———, "Singularities in Consecutive-Tense Constructions in the Isaiah Scroll," *VT*, V (1955), 180–188.

Rüthy, A. E., "Die Bedeutung biblischer Handschriftenfunds," *IKT*, XLIV (1954), 173–192.

Schoeps, H. J., "Das gnostische Judentum in den 'Dead Sea Scrolls,' " *ZRG*, VI (1954), 276–279.

Schubert, H., "Die Handschriftenfunde vom Toten Meer," *SKZ*, CXXII (1954), 39, 50–53, 65.

———, "Der Sektenkanon von En Feshcha und die Anfänge der jüdischen Gnosis," *TLZ*, LXXVIII (1953), col. 495–506.

Scott, R. B. Y., "Acquisition of Dead Sea Scroll Fragments by McGill University," *BASOR*, No. 135, Oct., 1954, 8.

Segal, M. H., "The Promulgation of the Authoritative Text of the Hebrew Bible," *JBL*, LXXII (1953), 35–47.

Segert, S., "Ein alter Bericht über den Fund hebräischer Handschriften in einer Höhle," *AO*, XXI (1953), 263–269.

———, "Zur Habakuk-Rolle aus dem Funde vom Toten Meer II," *AO*, XXII (1954), 99–113.

Sellers, O. R., "A Possible Old Testament Reference to the Teacher of Righteousness," *IEJ*, V (1955), 93–95.

Silberman, L. H., "The Two 'Messiahs' of the Manual of Discipline," *VT*, V (1955), 77–82.

Skehan, P. W., "Exodus in the Samaritan Recension from Qumran," *JBL*, LXXIV (1955), 182–187.

———, "A Fragment of the 'Song of Moses' (Deut. 32) from Qumran," *BASOR*, No. 136, Dec., 1954, 12–15.

———, "The Text of Isaias at Qumrān," *CBQ*, XVII (1955), 158–163 (38–43).

Solá Solé, J.M., "Una Tendencia lingüística en al manuscrito de Isaias (DSIa) de Khirbet Qumran," *Sef.*, XIII (1953), 61–72.

Sonne, I., "The X-Sign in the Isaiah Scroll," *VT*, IV (1954), 90–94.

Sparks, H. F. D., "Prof. Dupont-Sommer on the Discoveries by the Dead Sea," *MC*, XLIV (1954), 300–305.

Starcky, J., "Un Contrat nabatéen sur papyrus," *RB*, LXI (1954), 161–181.

Sukenik, E. L., *Osar Hammegilloth haggenuzoth*. Jerusalem: Bialik Institute, 1954.

Talmon, S., "The Sectarian *yḥd*—a Biblical Noun," *VT*, III (1953), 133–140.

Teicher, J. L., "Are the Bar Kokhba Documents Genuine?" *JJS*, V (1954), 38.

——, "The Christian Interpretation of the Sign X in the Isaiah Scroll," *VT*, V (1955), 189–198.

——, "Documents of the Bar-Kochba Period," *JJS*, IV (1953), 132–134.

——, "The Habakkuk Scroll," *JJS*, V (1954), 47–59.

——, "Jesus' Sayings in the Dead Sea Scrolls," *JJS*, V (1954), 38.

——, "Priests and Sacrifices in the DSS," *JJS*, V (1954), 93–99.

——, "Puzzling Passages in the Damascus Fragments," *JJS*, V (1954), 139–147.

——, "The Teaching of the Pre-Pauline Church in the Dead Sea Scrolls," *JJS*, IV (1953), 1–13, 49–58, 93–103, 139–153.

Trever, J. C., "Studies in the Problem of Dating the Dead Sea Scrolls," *Proc. Amer. Phil. Soc.*, XCVII (1953), 184–193.

de Vaux, R., "Exploration de la région de Qumrân," *RB*, LX (1953), 540–561.

——, "Fouille au Khirbet Qumrân: Rapport préliminaire," *RB*, LX (1953), 83–106.

——, "Fouilles au Khirbet Qumrân: Rapport préliminaire sur la deuxième campagne," *RB*, LXI (1954), 206–236.

——, "Les Grottes de Murabba'at et leurs documents," *RB*, LX (1953), 245–267.

——, "Quelques textes hébreux de Murabba'at," *RB*, LX (1953), 268–275.

Vermès, G., "A propos des commentaires bibliques découverts a Qumrān," *RHPR*, XXXV (1955), 95–103.

——, "Le Cadre historique des manuscrits de la Mer morte," *RSR*, XLI (1953), 5–29, 203–230.

——, *Les Manuscrits du Désert de Juda*. Tournai, 1953 (2nd ed., 1954).

Wallenstein, M., "A Hymn from the Scrolls," VT, V (1955), 277-283.

———, "Some Lexical Material in the Judean Scrolls," VT, IV (1954), 211-214.

Wernberg-Moeller, P., "Notes on the Manual of Discipline," VT, III (1953), 195-202.

———, "Observations on the Interchange of ' and ḥ in the Manual of Discipline," VT, III (1953), 104-107.

———, "Sdq, Sdyq and Sdwq in the Zadokite Fragments, the Manual of Discipline and the Habakkuk-Commentary," VT, III (1953), 310-315.

Wieder, N., "The Doctrine of the Two Messiahs Among the Karaites," JJS, VI (1955), 14-25.

———, "The Habakkuk Scroll and the Targum," JJS, IV (1953), 14-18.

———, "The 'Law-Interpreter' of the Sect of the Dead Sea Scrolls: The Second Moses," JJS, IV (1953), 158-175.

———, "The Term qṣ in the Dead Sea Scrolls and in Hebrew Liturgical Poetry," JJS, V (1954), 22-31.

Wiesenberg, E., "Chronological Data in the Zadokite Fragments," VT, V (1955), 284-308.

Wildberger, H., "Die 'Sectenrolle' vom Toten Meer," ET, XIII (1953), 25-43.

Winter, P., "Notes on Wieder's Observations on the dwrš htwrh in the Book of the New Covenanters of Damascus," JQR, XLV (1954), 39-47.

Yadin, Y., "A Note on DSD IV, 20," JBL, LXXIV (1955), 40-43.

Zeitlin, S., "The Antiquity of the Hebrew Scrolls and the Piltdown Hoax: A Parallel," JQR, XLV (1954), 1-29.

———, "The Essenes and Messianic Expectations," JQR, XLV (1954), 83-119.

———, "The Fiction of the Recent Discoveries near the Dead Sea," JQR, XLIV (1953), 85-115.

———, "A Note on the Fiction of the 'Bar Kokba' Letter," JQR, XLV (1954), 174-180.

———, "The Propaganda of the Hebrew Scrolls and the Falsification of History," JQR, XLVI (1955), 1-39.

Index

Aaron, 24, 62, 63, 74, 78, 82, 83, 115, 121
Abel, F. M., 2
Acts, Book of, 51, 117, 124
'Ain Feshka, 19
Albright, W. F., 31, 90
Alexander Jannaeus, 83
Alexandrian canon, 48
American School of Oriental Research, 27, 28, 32, 33, 35, 38
Ammon(ites), 36, 71
Andromache, 51
Anra Mainyu, 73
Antigonus Mattathias, 16
Apocryphal, vii, 34, 48, 57, 111
Aqiba, 47
Aquila, 59
Arab(s), vii, 19, 20, 28, 54, 55, 88
Arabia, 60
Arabic, 51, 55, 56, 59, 87
Aramaic, 30, 31, 34, 37, 40, 46, 49, 56, 60
Aramaism(s), 76
Archaeological Museum, 3, 26, 53. *See also* Palestine Museum
Aristobulus II, 83
Arius, 88
Assumption of Moses, 106

Baptism(al), 7, 66, 113–116
Bar Kokhba (Bar Koziba, or Ben Koziba; also, Simeon ben Kosiba), 58, 59
Barthélemy, D., 32, 59
Baumgartner, W., 48
Belial, 71, 72, 77, 114, 115, 125
 men of, 66
 kingdom of, 75

Benjamin, 35, 71
Beth Mashko, 58
Birnbaum, S. A., 31, 57, 58
al-Bīrūnī, 87
Book of Lamech, 34. *See also* "Lamech Scroll"
Book of Lights and Watch-Towers, 86
Braun, F. M., 127
Braun, O., 88
Brown, R. E., 127
Brownlee, W. H., 33, 34, 65, 74, 75, 77, 78, 83, 106, 112, 116, 117, 120, 122
Burrows, M., 32, 33, 79
Byzantine, 20, 51

Caesarea, 14, 17, 18, 19
Cairo Genizah Document of the Damascus Covenanters (CDC), 7, 20, 24, 32, 43, 46, 77, 79–87, 89, 108, 109, 111. See also *Fragments of a Zadokite Work*; Zadokite Document
Calendar, 46, 48, 68, 70, 85, 87
Cave 1 (1Q), 3, 13, 27, 28–38, 39, 40, 46, 47, 49, 56, 61, 71, 80, 89
Cave 1 (Mur), 52, 54, 56
Cave 2 (2Q), 27, 39, 40
Cave 2 (Mur), 52, 54, 56
Cave 3 (3Q), 27, 39, 40, 41, 49
Cave 3 (Mur), 52, 56
Cave 4 (4Q), 25, 27, 39, 43–46, 69
Cave 4 (Mur), 52, 56
Cave 5 (5Q), 27, 39, 43
Cave 6 (6Q), 28, 39, 43, 89
Cemetery, 1, 2, 3, 9, 13, 20, 104

Chalcolithic, 54
Charles, R. H., 8, 21, 76
Christian(s), 58, 62, 87, 88, 118, 119, 126
Christo-Palestinian, 51
Clermont-Ganneau, C., 2, 9, 10
Coins, 5, 12, 13, 14, 16, 17, 19, 20, 31, 39, 43, 55, 58
Colossians, 51
Communal meal(s), 65, 66, 67, 75, 84, 104, 105, 122, 123, 124
Community of the New Covenant, 21, 69, 109
Contracts, 56, 60
Conybeare, F. C., 118
Cook, K., 90
Copper scroll(s), 39, 41, 42, 49
Council, 63, 64, 120, 121
Covenant, New, 76, 77, 79, 81, 85
Covenant Community, 24, 74, 75, 81, 110, 122, 125
Covenanters (of Damascus), 76, 79, 80, 84-87, 110, 112, 114, 117, 120, 122, 125
Cross, F. M., Jr., 27, 44, 45, 46, 53

Dalman, G., 3
Damascus, 21, 22, 24, 76, 79, 81, 85
   Covenanters, 74, 79, 80, 81, 83, 84, 87, 104
   Sect, 76, 77, 84
Daniel, Book of, 37, 38, 45
David, 54, 55
Davies, W. D., 127
De Contenson, H., 39
De Langhe, R., 51
De Saulcy, F., 2
De Vaux, R., 3, 4, 6, 10, 11, 12, 15, 16, 20, 26, 27, 30, 31, 38 40, 41, 42, 43, 51, 53, 55, 56, 57, 58, 59, 88
Delcor, M., 122
Department of Antiquities (Jordan), 3, 26, 43, 53
Deuteronomy, 30, 40, 45, 57
Didachē, 72
Dio Chrysostom, 91
Dora, 14, 19
Driver, G. R., 88
Dualism, 71-73, 117, 118

Dupont-Sommer, A., 11, 68, 73, 82, 91, 106, 108, 109, 110, 115, 118, 119

Earthquake, 6, 9, 12, 14, 17, 19, 20
Ebionite, 112
École Biblique, 3, 26, 38, 43. See also French Archaeological School
Edom(ites), 36, 71
Egypt, 88
Eisler, R., 112
Elliger, K., 34
Engedi, 54, 91
Enoch, Book of, 31, 46, 48, 70, 72, 85, 106, 107
Ephesus, 117
Essene(s), 8, 11, 22, 23, 24, 46, 62, 64, 66, 67, 74, 90-110, 112, 113, 116, 117, 118, 120, 122, 123, 124, 125
Esther, Book of, 45, 74
Euripides, 51
Eusebius, 94
Exodus, Book of, 30, 40, 57

Fourth Gospel. See John, Gospel of
Fragments of a Zadokite Work, 7, 21. See also Cairo Genizah, etc.; Zadokite Document
French Archaeological School, 53. See also École Biblique

Gabinius, 50
Galileans, 58
Gärtner, B., 127
Genesis, 30, 49, 57, 59
Ginsberg, H. L., 58, 122
Ginsburg, C. D., 118
Gnostic, 74, 118
Gomorrah, 2
Greek(s), 12, 13, 22, 30, 48, 50, 51, 56, 59, 60, 101, 102, 125
   Translation, 47, 48, 111. See also Septuagint
   Version, 40
Grossouw, W., 127

Habakkuk, Book of, 34, 47, 59
Habakkuk Commentary (1QpHab), 20, 32, 33, 34, 36, 37, 74, 77, 81, 82, 83, 106

Hadrian, 55, 57, 58
Hagu, Book of, 32, 80
Hajar al-Asbah, 27, 38
Harding, G. Lankester, 3, 26, 53
Hasidim, 70, 83
Hasmonean, 14, 16, 50, 83
Hebrew, 13, 30, 31, 32, 33, 34, 37,
  40, 42, 45, 46, 47, 48, 56, 57, 58,
  59, 60, 76, 88, 111, 125
  alphabet, 12, 56
  archaic, 34, 40, 45, 49, 56
  University, 28, 29, 32, 34, 35
Hellenistic, 12, 13, 30, 47
Herod (the Great), 14, 17, 20, 22,
  23, 24, 50, 79, 106, 110
Herod Antipas, 22
Herod Archelaus, 14, 17, 20
Hodayoth (1QH), 47. *See also*
  Thanksgiving Hymns
Holy Spirit, 67, 108, 115, 121
Howie, C. G., 127
Hvidberg, H. H., 76
Hyksos, 54
Hyrcania, 50
Hyrcanus, John (I), 14, 16, 19, 20
  (II), 23

Idumea(n), 18, 22
Iranian, 73, 118
Iron Age II, 16, 54
Isaiah, Book of, 40, 45, 46, 47, 57,
  120, 121, 122
Isaiah Scroll (1QIs^a), 32, 33, 34, 37,
  38, 47, 120
  (1QIs^b), 35, 37, 47
Israel(ite), 16, 19, 21, 24, 29, 32,
  37, 58, 60, 62, 63, 64, 67, 69, 70,
  74, 78, 79, 82, 83, 85, 108, 112,
  113, 114, 115, 121, 122, 123

Jeremiah, Book of, 40, 45
Jesus, 112, 116, 117, 118, 119, 120,
  122, 123
Jew(s), 19, 21, 22, 28, 36, 71, 72, 74,
  76, 88, 110, 113, 114
Jewish, 11, 14, 19, 20, 22, 23, 31, 37,
  55, 56, 57, 58, 59, 60, 72, 83, 86,
  88, 106, 110, 114, 118, 119, 122
  Revolt, First, 14, 17, 57
  Revolt, Second, 5, 14, 19, 20, 47,
  55, 56, 57, 58, 59, 60

John, Gospel of, 51, 116, 117
John the Baptist, 22, 112–117
Jonah, Book of, 59
Josephus, 6, 8, 11, 17, 18, 24, 64,
  66, 67, 91, 97, 103–110, 112, 116,
  122, 123
Joshua, Book of, 51
Jubilees, Book of, 30, 31, 40, 41, 46,
  48, 70, 72, 85, 87, 106, 107
  Year of, 70
Judaea Capta, 14, 19
Judaeo-Christian, 112
Judah, 21, 35, 71
Judaism, 70, 73, 85, 90, 103, 111,
  118
Judea(n), 26, 60, 81, 104, 112
  Desert, viii, 28, 50, 52
  Wilderness, vii
Judges, Book of, 30

Kahle, P., 30, 89
Karaites, 21, 86, 89
Kastellion, 50, 51
Khirbet (al) Mird, 28, 50, 51
Kirkisānī, 86, 87, 89
Kittim, 36, 71, 83
Kuhn, K. G., 41, 42, 73, 118, 123,
  124, 125

Lachish, 56
Lambert, G., 33
"Lamech Scroll," 49. *See also* **Book**
  of Lamech
Latin, 56, 57
Lawgiver, 81
Letter of Barnabas, 72
Level I, II, III (Qumrān), 12, 13,
  14, 19
Levi, 35, 46, 63, 71
Levites, 65, 66, 72, 78, 79
Leviticus, 30, 31, 40, 56
Lightfoot, J. B., 118
Lord's Supper, 122, 123, 124
Luke, Gospel of, 35, 51

Maccabean, 31, 37, 47, 72, 83, 90,
  109
Mader, E., 51
Magharians, 87
Malachi, Book of, 46, 47
Man of Lies, 77, 81, 83

Manual of Discipline (1KS), 7, 11,
31–34, 61, 62, 66, 67, 69, 70, 72,
73, 77, 79, 80, 81, 84, 85, 86, 104,
105, 108, 109, 117, 118, 123
Many, The, 63, 64, 65, 77, 79, 105,
119
Mar Athanasius Y. Samuel, 29, 32
Mar Saba, 50
Marcus, R., 74
Margoliouth, G., 111
Mark, Gospel of, 51
Masada, 91
Masoretic text (M), 33, 38, 40, 45,
47, 48
tradition, 33, 34, 37, 40, 47, 57
Matthew, Gospel of, 51
mebaqqer, 63, 77, 80, 81, 84, 104
Mesopotamia, 90
Messiah, 24, 67, 74, 78, 81, 83, 88,
113, 114, 115, 116, 120, 121, 122,
123
Messianic, 22, 23, 32, 46, 67, 75, 81,
82, 114, 116, 120, 122, 123
Age, 24, 81, 121
Micah, Book of, 59
Middle Bronze Age, 54
Midrash, 74
Milik, J. T., 2, 30, 46, 51, 58, 60
Minor Prophets, 59
Mishnaic, 76
Moab(ites), 36, 71
Moses, 61, 74, 81, 114
Mowry, L., 127
Muḥammad Dib, 28
Muilenburg, J., 45
Murabba'at, 28, 46, 48, 49, 51–59
Museum of Antiquities (Jerusalem,
Israel), 35

Nabatean(s), 17, 60
Nahum, Book of, 59
Nemoy, L., 86, 87
Nero, 14, 18, 55
New Testament, 48, 88, 111, 112,
118, 122, 124, 125
New York *Times*, 29, 49
North, R., 2, 24, 28
Numbers, Book of, 40, 59

Old Testament, vii, 30, 35, 38, 45,
46, 47, 73, 74, 88, 111

Origen, 30, 59
Overseer, 9, 63, 64. *See also* Supervisor

Palestine Museum (Jerusalem, Jordan), viii, 5, 26, 31, 38, 41, 43,
44
Palestinian-Jewish, 118
Palimpsest, 56
Papyrus, 56, 57, 60
Paqîd, 63
Paraclete, 117
Passover, 124
Paul, 112, 125–127
Pentateuch, 45
Pesher(s), 30, 33, 46, 47
Peter, 123
Pharisaic-Rabbinic, 118
Pharisee(s), 22, 23, 74, 85, 87, 97,
103, 113, 118, 119
Philistines, 71
Philo, 90, 91, 94, 103–110
Phylactery, 46, 57, 59
Pliny, 90, 91, 104
Pompey, 50
Priest(s), 8, 61, 62, 63, 64, 65, 67,
72, 78, 79, 80, 81, 83, 120,
123
Prophet(s), 46, 61, 73, 74, 78, 81,
85, 106, 108, 119, 122
Psalms, Book of, 35, 40, 45, 46, 47,
59, 88
Pseudepigrapha, 85
Pseudepigraphical, 48, 111

Qoheleth, 45
Quinta, 59

Rabbanites, 87
Rabbinic, 70
Rabin, C., 76
Rabinowitz, I., 21, 31
Rabinowitz, J. J., 58
Radiocarbon test, 29
Ras Feshka, 2, 27, 38
Reed, W. L., 27, 38
Reservoir(s), 5, 6, 7, 9, 66, 105
Roman(s), 1, 3, 5, 9, 13, 14, 17, 18,
19, 20, 25, 30, 37, 42, 52, 55, 56,
57, 58, 59, 83, 109
Tenth Legion, 4, 14, 17, 18, 19

Rost, L., 76
Rowley, H. H., 31, 89
Ruth, Book of, 40

Sadducees, 87, 97, 103, 113, 118
I Samuel, 45, 46
Schechter, S., 20, 21, 76, 80, 85, 86, 87
Schürer, E., 58
Scriptorium, 4, 5
Seleucids, 36, 71
Sellers, O. R., 27, 29
Septuagint (LXX), 45, 46, 48. See under Greek
Serek, 77
Sergius, 88
Servant Songs, 120, 122
Shahrastānī, 88
Shemaʿ, 57
Simeon ben Kosiba, 58, 59, 60. See also Bar Kokhba
Skehan, P. W., 45
Sōd, 62, 120
Sodom, 91
Sonne, I., 74
Spenta Mainyu, 73
Star, 21, 46, 76, 81
Starcky, J., 60
Suffering Servant, 120, 121, 122
Sukenik, E. L., 34, 35, 37
Supervisor, 9, 14, 62, 63, 65, 77, 80, 84, 104, 108, 124. See also Overseer
Symmachus, 59
Synesius, 91
Syria, 50
Syriac, 51, 88, 90
Syrian Archbishop, 37. See also Mar Athanasius
Syrian Orthodox Convent, 28, 29, 32, 34

Taʿamireh, 27, 28, 50, 51, 53, 55
Talmudic, 76
Teacher of Righteousness, 20, 74, 77, 81, 82, 83, 109, 112, 119, 127
Teicher, J. L., 112
Temple (Jerusalem), 83, 84, 108, 109
Ten Commandments, 46

Tenth Legion. See under Roman
Testaments of the Twelve Patriarchs, 72, 106, 107
Testimonia, 46
Tetragrammaton, 34
Thanksgiving Hymns, 35. See also Hodayoth
Theodotion, 59
Timotheus I, 88, 89
Titus, 18, 19
Tobit, Book of, 46
Torrey, C. C., 31
Trever, J. C., 34
Two Ways, 72

Unique Teacher, 81, 82
Uzziah, 16

Vallois, H. V., 10
Vermès, G., 127
Vespasian, 17, 18, 19

Wadi Daraja, 52
Qumrān, 1, 39, 46, 66
War of the Children of Light Against the Children of Darkness (1QM), 23, 35, 71, 72, 75, 109, 125
Scroll. See above
Wicked Priest, 81, 83
Wisdom of Solomon, Book of, 51
Women, 10, 11, 32, 62, 104
Wright, G. E., 37, 38

X (sign), 14, 18, 19

Yahad, 61, 62
Yeivin, S., 31
Yeshua ben Galgola, 58

Zadok, 87
Sons of, 75, 76, 77, 79, 87
Zadokite(s), 87
Document, 21, 22, 28, 44, 76. See also Cairo Genizah Document; Fragments of a Zadokite Work
Zealots, 56, 109
Zechariah, Book of, 59
Zeitlin, S., 76, 86
Zephaniah, Book of, 59
Zoroastrianism, 73